Dear Karen,

May you know & nourish
that which is real within
you... :)

Blessings!

25/7/13

AWAKEN
OUR SPIRIT WITHIN

A Journey of Self-Realization and Transformation

Patsie Smith

Shrivatsa (Sanskrit)
The Endless Knot

BALBOA
PRESS
A DIVISION OF HAY HOUSE

Balboa Press books may be ordered through booksellers or by contacting:

Balboa Press
A Division of Hay House
1663 Liberty Drive
Bloomington, IN 47403
www.balboapress.com.au
1-(877) 407-4847

ISBN: 978-1-4525-0728-6 (sc)
ISBN: 978-1-4525-0729-3 (e)

Because of the dynamic nature of the Internet, any web addresses or links contained in this book may have changed since publication and may no longer be valid. The views expressed in this work are solely those of the author and do not necessarily reflect the views of the publisher, and the publisher hereby disclaims any responsibility for them.

The author of this book does not dispense medical advice or prescribe the use of any technique as a form of treatment for physical, emotional, or medical problems without the advice of a physician, either directly or indirectly. The intent of the author is only to offer information of a general nature to help you in your quest for emotional and spiritual well-being. In the event you use any of the information in this book for yourself, which is your constitutional right, the author and the publisher assume no responsibility for your actions.

Cover image and design © Jessica Smith.
Book illustrations © Elaine Smith.
Cover photos by Patsie Smith: Ice waterfall, Nepal Himalaya.

Printed in the United States of America

Balboa Press rev. date: 02/06/2013

To my beautiful, beloved children, James, Jessica, and Elaine:

Thank you for continuing to be the most significant part of my life, for all that we share, and for all that I continue to learn through each of you. It is a privilege to be able to share your exciting and unique life journeys. Thank you for the ups and downs, laughter and tears, frustrations and challenges, joys, warmth, and love. There is no greater reward and joy in the journey of life than the role of a mother. Material life and pursuits come and go, but to live true to our spirit is a gift that I hope as a mother I can impart to you in this lifetime. With all my love.

To my uncle Pok Yong and aunty Marcelle:

May you find peace and strength and grow in spirit on your healing journeys.

To all who seek the ultimate truth of their own reality and who are on the path of inner growth toward true freedom from suffering and transcendence into ultimate inner peace.

THE INNATE LONGING WITHIN EVERY soul is to awaken from the spirit's slumber and then to journey home.

—Patsie Smith

Contents

Preface

THIS BOOK CONVEYS IN MY voice the echo of truth in line with what has been expounded by many enlightened masters. I have not led a monastic life or been tutored in any particular belief system. All that I have learned has been a gift bestowed by life itself simply by having an open heart, staying true to my spirit, and making conscious choices through paths of the heart. All practical learning has been a gift through the guidance and words of many awakened souls that have come before and with me.

My spiritual journey of self-learning and self-healing has spanned the last twenty-seven years. Typically my lessons in life have first come as experience, then soon afterward, life would magically bring along a book that seemed to explain those experiences. Such has been my journey of direct learning. I have also undertaken retreats and workshops over those years, from yogic science to shamanism, and delved into many forms of meditation. At all times I was open, learned and took what felt right, then moved on. I remained a masterless student, learning from all but attached to none. Life continues to be a journey of endless learning.

I do not have a string of impressive writing credentials. I have not previously authored any books or attended writing courses or workshops. I never had any conscious intention of writing a book. The extent of my writing experience has been in my personal journals and a blog where I share with like-minded souls. I did no specific or extensive theoretical research in writing this book. All the contents derive from a natural culmination of my practical learning through direct life experiences in line with application of wisdom taught by enlightened masters, from His Holiness the Fourteenth Dalai Lama to Meister Eckhart Tolle. Along my learning journey, I have explored all areas of spiritualism, from Buddhism to quantum science of consciousness. They all convey and point to the same inner truth, just through different interpretations. Some major literature that contributed profoundly to my growth and learning can be found under "Recommended Reading."

My work as a remedial massage therapist and yoga/meditation teacher over the last decade has exposed me to a variety of human physical, emotional, and mental states. Clients who have confided in me and sought my guidance with their life issues have taught me just as much as they may have learned from me. Through them, I have learned extensively about the state of the human spirit and the mind-body-spirit connection in human existence. These insights have also contributed to the contents of this book.

Over the years of healing and learning, major shifts in my levels of consciousness were accompanied by profound mystical experiences. Initially, I was prompted to start writing down these experiences and this wisdom for my children to help them on their life journeys. But it was a stop-start project that did not flow smoothly. Then in 2011, I was privileged to have the profound experience of dissolution of my limited self. That experience was unlike any other and was indescribable in words until the manuscript for this book came about in July 2012. Words would flow through me while I was working, cleaning the house, driving, running, or walking my dog and were interrupted only by my routine chores and duties and physical limitations. There would be nights when my eyelids would shut while I was halfway through typing a sentence. The words started to take shape into a manuscript and have a life of their own. This book contains profound messages that come from that realm beyond the physical. Every word is meant to be shared with all. I am merely the vessel.

Acknowledgments

To my ex-husband, Andrew:

THANK YOU FOR SHARING TWENTY-FOUR years of my life and contributing toward my spirit's endless journey of healing and learning. I hope that you will find it in your heart to be at peace with me one day over the ending of our partnership. We are destined to honor our spirits' journey. May you come to learn that what is truly real is immaterial. May you awaken and realize your own true peace and unconditional love.

To all the dear and beautiful souls who share and are a part of my life as family, friends, partners, teachers, students, and clients:

Thank you for being in the path of my discovery, growth, learning, and enrichment toward my journey home.

Thank you to my editor, Liz Rehfeldt. Also, to the editorial and publishing team at Balboa Press, thank you for your high professional, technical and quality standards, in helping me get this book into the hands and hearts of all.

Thank you to these awakened/enlightened souls/masters who have been a profound source of inspiration and truth to me through their lives, teachings, words, wisdom, and purity of being:

Gautama Buddha
Jesus Christ
Lao Tzu
His Holiness the Fourteenth Dalai Lama
Sri Ramana Maharshi
Mooji
Jalaluddin Rumi
Meister Eckhart Tolle
Gabriel Cousens
Jack Kornfield
Nelson Mandela

Introduction

THIS BOOK CONTAINS WORDS FROM a place deep within us all that you will recognize when you are still and quiet. Read and listen with your hearts, not your thinking brain. Our analytical, logical, objective brain is limited in the realm of the spirit, and the contents of this book are not theories, concepts, beliefs, or logic borne out of the human brain. This is not a textbook, a novel, or a psychology or self-help book. Be still, listen with your heart, and let your spirit recognize, reveal, and awaken itself.

This is a "living" book. If you do not understand or relate to certain sections, set the book aside, keep your hearts and senses open, and life will reveal itself in due course. Return to the book, if and when compelled to do so, and the words will take on a different depth, allowing new understanding. An awakened soul once said, "If our consciousness is the size of a pea, we can only understand the extent of a pea. If our consciousness is the size of an ocean, we will understand the extent of an ocean." Our level of understanding of matters of the spirit depends on our level of consciousness.

The essence of this book is not new; many have trod the awakened path and many are on it. Many books have been written, words spoken, and teachings given, all pointing toward the same truth. Reading this book while remaining in the spirit, you may arrive through innate knowing at a sense of connection, familiarity, and inner realization that may cause a shift into a higher and expanded state. It is also normal if parts of this book evoke certain reactions, objections, and resistance. This book was not written to make huge profits or to appease every single reader. You may encounter words that challenge a false sense of self. Words of truth from the spirit will often confront the ego self of mind, identity, and beliefs. As such, at the end of every chapter, I have added a reflection: the opportunity to stop, be still, and allow the noise of the mind, ego, and identity to quiet down. For it is in silence that our spirit and truth are revealed.

The main body of this book was naturally and intentionally written mostly in the first person plural. Although nonconforming by literary standards, it is significant because it connotes our oneness. It is the voice that feels right and natural for the purpose of this book, since our reality is on a unified plane. The *we* and *us* throughout the book engage you the reader as another unified part of me and all others. However, I switch to the second person narrative when I engage you the reader as an individual in active participation in sections where I guide or instruct in reflection and meditation.

This book can be read in its entirety in one go, but is more effective if you take your time to read, reflect in quiet for the insights, and apply the awareness to your daily life. It can be read again at varying points, and its significance may change in depth as may your understanding. In my twenties, before I had awakened to my spirit, when I first read *The Tao Te Ching* by Lao Tzu, I could not comprehend at all what was being conveyed. When I first read *How to See Yourself as You Really Are* by His Holiness the Fourteenth Dalai Lama, nothing made sense, and I had to put the book aside. Fifteen years later, reading the same book, I found myself understanding with ease all the words because they were my personal reality. The works of Persian poet Jalalludin Rumi bring tears to my eyes because they speak from the heart and soul as if they were my own words.

Although the past is insignificant since the present moment is our only true reality, I honor the past to the extent that it has led to where I am today. Thus I include autobiographical accounts in some sections to share experiences that may enhance the understanding of messages conveyed. In sharing accounts of my personal journey, I empathize with the depths of human suffering common to us all. But significantly this highlights the choice for transcendence that is possible for all of us when we awaken and live our spirit's path. This book is divided into part 1 before awakening and part 2 after awakening to portray clearly the big picture of the beautiful path toward living as an awakened spirit.

In this book, the word *spirit* is used to connote our true self, life, and the presence within us that is beyond our flesh, bones, and mind. Other spiritual books and teachers may point to this reality with terms like *higher self, universal self, God, Buddha within, consciousness, Christ consciousness, essence,* or *core.* The word *soul* in this book refers to our complete inner and outer self in this life journey. The terms *limited self, small self,* and *ego* are used to denote our limited physical human self. *Spiritual journey* and *spiritualism* in this book refer to our spirit's journey in its pure sense, before affiliations with any religion, ideology, or belief system.

Finally, the intention of this book is not to convince or convert readers or to promote any kind of belief system. Do not take my word or anyone else's at face value. Discern the truth of the words in this book for yourself with your own innate intuition. As the Buddha said, "Be a light unto yourself," and as Zen Master Rinzai said, "Place no head above your own." May the words of this book speak to all hearts and souls.

PART 1

Before Awakening

CHAPTER 1

What Is Awakening?

AWAKENING IS DEFINED AS A rousing or a quickening, and generally, to awaken is to arise from a sleep or dormancy. So it is not a discovery or acquisition of something new or foreign, but an awakening to our true self, which is already present. This is an awakening of our spirit (which is already there and is us) from the natural slumber to which it is subject throughout human existence. In the journey of human existence, the inevitable acquiring of many layers gives us a physical identity and personality. On such a course, we may end up shielding our spirit, our pure and true self. So shielded is our spirit that it appears to be in slumber as we lose our connection with it and, like many, completely forget about it. So our journey of awakening begins with peeling back these layers to our core.

To convey this plight of our shielded human spirit, let's explore further by asking ourselves, what am I?

To answer this question, let's journey back to the point of our birth. When we were born, we emerged out of our mothers into this physical world as screaming, crying newborn babies or maybe quiet, slightly blue ones for a short while. Nevertheless, we finally took our first breaths in this world. We were pure life in the form of a human newborn, no different from a pure life that emerged out of a chicken egg or a horse, just different in appearance and physiology. All the cells in this pure living being sprang to life. Our organs kick-started, the heart pumped itself, the lungs took in and expelled air, and our little digestive systems started to process the nourishing mother's milk. We could move; we kicked our legs, writhed, and opened and shut our eyelids. We yawned, cried, screamed at the top of our lungs, and instinctively started to feed to grow.

What is this pure living energy surging through a newborn human being? Like a television plugged into a socket with the power turned on, so too we are just pure life energy propelled into and through a physical form. Then within a few days or weeks, we were given a name. With that, we had the start of an identity. Our identity continued to build. Our family name, history, and racial background brought along with them a set of traditions and culture that we grew into over the proceeding years. The geographical and natural environment in which we grew up helped shape us in the growing years. Our day-to-day life experiences also had their effect. Our human brain with its amazing capabilities started firing, wiring, and establishing connections from the moment of birth based on all the experiences filtering in through our five senses.

The nurturing and love we received or did not receive from our parents or caregivers, the pleasant or unpleasant, joyful or traumatic experiences of events and people started to form our personality, character, thought patterns, outlook, and opinions. Once we started to speak words in a language, we could communicate and think in words. Further on, education, religion, and societal expectations continued to shape us. This cycle continued to build more layers, one on top of the other, as our lives continued. The human brain, the most developed on earth, has the capacity for memory, submemory, conditioning, feelings, analysis, and reasoning, and so it continues to store and build what we perceive as our selves.

The journey to know who we are starts with awakening to that pure, true original life that we started off with. Peel off those layers that we have allowed to build on us through life, and there we are, in spirit. It may sound simple, but for many, this process is not easy to see or carry out. The stark reality of who we are beyond the physical and material confronted me years ago during the wet lab component of my studies on human anatomy and physiology for massage therapy training.

Working on cadavers, it became amazingly obvious how blind we are to the reality that without the living spirit, the corpse is just a piece of dead meat. The human race bases its whole existence, with its false sense of self and limited life span, on this piece of meat. All of life revolves around protecting, sustaining, and defining this limited anatomy of flesh and bones. Where is the focus on the real—that which is not born and does not die, which does not decay, but merely transforms, that which is unseen, the quiet and not all the noise?

Each individual's awakening experience is unique; some are gradual, others spontaneous. Some may be earth-shaking, others quietly sublime. Awakening is an experiential reality accompanied by a shift in our inner consciousness. Generally, most awakening experiences have been described as beyond words, sublime peace, joy, beauty, love, and bliss. Awakening is not a mental concept to be grasped. It cannot be faked, learned, or forced. When our spirit awakens, it is a personal reality that naturally brings about changes on every level of our lives.

Those of us who have awakened to the reality of our spirit look further within ourselves. Before birth, where was I? Who and what was I? Before birth, we were life in the womb. Before life in the womb, what/ who was I? Some know that before and underneath our physical form we are just pure energy, and they look further. Where does the energy come from? If we consist purely of energy, that energy must emanate from somewhere. We can still perceive and experience energy that is us, so we must be beyond energy. The depth of learning and discovery is infinite, like the expanse of our outer universe. While there is a logical answer to the question of who we truly are, there is still a journey. When we ultimately learn what we truly are, it cannot be described in words. It is quite possible, however, to convey what or who we are not.

This poem flowed through me during one of my early morning jogs around the river. These are words from our true self, our pure spirit.

I Am

I am Life,
your pure essence, spirit, and seed of existence itself
that lies within you,
longing to awaken and flourish.

I am long before you and after you,
never born, never die,
timeless, without boundaries.

I am pure, unconditional love, wholeness,
connectedness, freedom, bliss, joy, peace, stillness.
I am That beyond the gross and limited,
yet you are blinded.
You choose the illusion
that you have control
through grasping and being caught
by all that is unreal and comes and goes.
You think you are alive,
but you barely know Life.
You choose separation.

It is time to wake up!
Have strength, courage, and trust to let go.
Surrender the fear
and all that imprisons you.

I am beyond mind, thoughts, emotions,
ego, conditioning, desires, needs, attachments,
memories, dreams, goals, forms, identities, ideas.
Beyond all that arises.
When all that I am not is released and let go,
I Am.

Many just glimpse and dismiss.
Trust and go all the way.
Stay in That which is still and unmoving,
watching and allowing
cutting, peeling, learning,
and the maturity naturally and totally unfolds.
Trust in your awakening
until the final curtain draws.
The illusion, limited, fragmented, contracted,
is totally dissolved and evaporated.

The ultimate and unbound freedom and effortlessness.
No more maintaining, seeking,
searching, finding, growing, getting,
coming, and going.
No more striving, battling, fixing, struggling.
No more ifs, buts, when, where, how.
No more in or out.
No more fear.
No more living life, just Life.
Pure, natural, infinite wholeness spills over.
All is fresh, spontaneous, alive, spirited
—limitless, pure beauty.
All else just debris for dusting off.

Seeing without eyes
Tasting without tongue
Hearing without ears
Touching without hands
Moving without feet.

Total, whole, eternal, infinite
And such also is all that arises.
No more questions. Home.
No more you, I, us.
No more words.

The next few paragraphs recount some of my awakening journeys thus far in life. I don't care very much about my past, since the present is our only true reality. However, my past has brought me to where I am today. In sharing some of my life journey, my aim is to show that, like most human beings, I have been entrapped in the web of suffering. This lifetime is only one of way too many that I have decided to experience for the evolution of my soul. My life experiences have included a dysfunctional childhood and depression in teenage and young adult years that led to an attempt at ending my life and coming face to face with death in my early twenties. Total lack of self-worth led to a dependence on people and later alcohol. My husband of nineteen years before our marriage ended was my crutch in life, and alcohol crept in quietly through the back door.

After the suicide attempt in my early twenties, something within me was profoundly shaken and shifted. I began a journey of searching, learning, healing, making mistakes, exploring, and opening up. I read every self-help and spiritual book I could lay my hands on. I explored Christianity (born-again and Catholicism) and a range of Eastern religions and philosophies. I undertook a major journey in self-healing including new age workshops in rebirthing, inner child work, African drumming, qigong, yoga, and various types of meditation. I was a lost soul who had ventured into the dark depths of despair. However, being so lost also spurred me into a series of awakenings and growth toward my spirit's ultimate freedom. My spirit's path remains a journey of endless profound realizations and continuous letting go of attachments to all that is not real.

A passionate involvement in martial arts in my young adult years led to internal energy arts, the path that most resonated with my soul. Hence, in my thirties and forties while fulfilling the role of a mother, caregiver, and dutiful wife, I was also learning yoga and yogic science, qigong, and especially meditation. This led to an initial awakening at about age thirty when in one of my personal chi (energy) meditations, I was privileged to experience the reality of nothingness. I lost all sense perceptions of my physical body. I was just pure energy, tingling and buzzing in expansion and vastness.

After that experience, when all that I had read and heard about our being pure energy became my personal reality, nothing was the same again. Experiencing the reality of pure energy dissolved all physical boundaries. Besides a peace beyond words, I suddenly felt a profound sense of connection to all living things, from strangers in the streets to the smallest ant. My daily life moved to a different level. I carried within me that "ball" of peace through all the ups and downs of life. It was my focus and anchor in life, and I was sustained by constant meditation. Sometimes in challenging and traumatic times, the ball of peace would shrink to the size of a pebble, but I was always able to inflate it again through consistent meditation.

At forty-five, having grown and matured, my spirit was strong. However, I felt a need to venture further within. I meditated with Zen monks, looked into more written work by spiritual souls, often sat up into the early morning hours listening to satsangs online with Mooji, and meditated even more. One day after a lovely morning meditation and yoga, I was doing my day's work with immense peace, when suddenly, something profoundly mystical happened subtly on the inside. Even as I was giving a client a bodywork treatment, fully awake and conscious, a sudden profound inner realization led to a most extraordinary experience. I felt myself disappear and had to pinch myself to see if I was dreaming. There was no me. I could not sense a physical me or my ball of peace, absolutely nothing. Then I experienced a flood of fear that persisted for the rest of the day and all that night. There was immeasurable fear, but there was no me. I was nonexistent, and all that was left was pure fear. I stayed with the fear, allowed and watched it, since I knew somehow this too would pass.

After sleeping with that fear, I awoke the next morning fresh, light, and renewed. Over the next few weeks, magical and mystical experiences continued. I did not feel like the same person, yet I was. I did not have that ball of peace anymore. In fact, I was peace itself, no shape, all encompassing. For months, I woke up every morning in disbelief. *Is it still here?* I would ask, and I couldn't help but wonder, *What did I do to deserve this?* I felt no distinction between the inside and outside of me, because there was no more door between the two. It felt like the end of all comings and goings, sometimes having "it" and sometimes losing "it." I had no more questions, just the pure feeling of being home.

Everything and everyone looked and felt different, from a single blade of grass on the ground to a flock of birds in the air. I was them and they were me. Then the path of life took another turn, and I found myself unable to speak or put anything into words until the birth of this book, which formed the words on its own within a span of two months. Nothing is the same anymore. I don't seem to live as a fragment in an illusion but as the whole. My spirit does not get bigger or smaller. It is not sometimes the foreground and other times the background. The background is now the total ground. All of life is a meditation. It is most difficult to describe.

These are my awakening experiences. Our spiritual journeys and awakenings are personal and unique to us alone, as individual as our fingerprints. Such is the beauty and gift of our spirit.

Reflection

Find time to be quiet with yourself every day, even if it is for just five to ten minutes. This quiet time means sitting and doing nothing at all—no music, television, reading, writing, or talking. Keep your eyes open without focusing on anything or keep them shut. If you know how to meditate, enter that space of stillness within. If you have never meditated, you may wish to try the breath meditation technique in the appendix of this book.

In the quietude, notice what it feels like within your body, underneath your skin, in your flesh, in your cells. Note all sensations and keep your presence within your body. If the mind wanders and gets distracted by thoughts, keep returning the focus to within your body. While you are fully present in your body, reflect on the words in this chapter with your heart. Do not analyze with your brain. Look within, feel, and ask, what am I and where is my spirit? But do not answer with your mind. Just sit with that question inside yourself.

CHAPTER 2

Why Awaken?

WE HAVE A CRUCIAL NEED to rise above ignorance and fear by awakening to our true selves and then honoring our spirit's journey toward ultimate freedom. On every level and for every reason, the need to awaken is our innate purpose. His Holiness the Fourteenth Dalai Lama presents the state of humankind and the nature of our spirit in a beautiful poem, "The Paradox of Our Age." Humankind, both at the personal and global levels, is in dire need of a turning point.

On a personal level, we have only to look at ourselves and people we know and love. How many people do we know who are struggling, suffering, and searching for peace? Are we truly happy? Do we even know what true happiness is? Why not? If we have the opportunity to awaken to true happiness, peace, and fulfillment, why would we not choose to do so? Our spirit longs to awaken, grow, and learn in pursuit of its ultimate realization. Physical, emotional, and mental dysfunctions continue to grow; depression and anxiety are the underlying cause of the

Western world's plight. Depression, suicide rates, eating disorders, and drug and alcohol abuse continue to rise every year. We can ignore the root of our plight and choose to be prescribed loads of drugs to mask the symptoms. We can sit around for years psychoanalyzing our past and present and plotting a desired future. We can read endless self-help and positive thinking books, which provide aid and inspiration. But ultimately, regardless of the techniques, therapies, and theories, nothing will be sustainable if we do not awaken to our spirit, our true self.

On a global level, we need only turn on the television or radio, read the newspapers, or simply look around our neighborhoods. There is widespread violence, anger, destruction, and abuse of our own kind, other life species, and nature itself, all with roots in greed, fear, and anxiety. Globally, it is crucial that we wake up for the betterment of our world and the evolution of our consciousness.

To get to the root of our plight, we need to wake up from our spirit's slumber. At some point in life, nearly everyone asks, *What am I? Who am I? What am I here for? How can I be happy, fulfilled, at peace? How can I stop the pain, struggling, and fear?* For some, these questions come early and for some later. But sooner or later, we start to question and seek, some from a young age when our lives confront us with trauma and major challenges that strip us of comfort and security. We are exposed to the rawness and jaggedness of this physical life from which emerges the longing for understanding and transcendence.

Others may reach this point at middle age. With half our lives gone, caught up in routines and monotony, having conformed to society's expectations, and fulfilled all cultural, material, and filial duties, we ask ourselves, *is this all there is?* Why is there still a sense of lacking or a longing for something beyond? Then there are those of us who live the illusion, oblivious and engrossed in ourselves and our possessions until we are confronted one day with the issue of life, suffering, and mortality. This could happen, for example, after we are diagnosed with an illness, we experience a tragedy, or death approaches for ourselves or a loved one. We are then confronted with the fragility of life and the impermanence of our physical selves and our physical world. This is when we start to wonder, search, and question.

This is when people may turn to groups, beliefs, and religions. Humans are collective and tribal beings. There is comfort, security, and a sense of purpose in following, belonging to, and identifying with a group beyond the immediate nuclear family. As such, we often choose to give a belief system, religion, group, organization, or culture our faith and loyalty in return for security and a sense of purpose and belonging. All major religions originated from the essence of divinity and universal love. However, we have shaped them into packages of beliefs, teachings, and rituals based on continents, races, and cultures. This has led to divisions among religions and belief systems.

The challenge for those involved in any religion or belief system is to keep it pure. When we lose or lack connection with the essence of religion, individual egos and attachments creep in, playing on human fears, insecurity, greed, and desires and producing divisions, power plays, anger, and hate. Many wars have been fought and lives sacrificed in the name of religion. Ultimately, humankind is of the same species, regardless of how we dress, speak, and look and regardless of how we believe. So if we have forgotten or deviated from our essence of divinity and universal love, it is imperative that we awaken to our core spirit.

Others who do not seek to conform or need to belong might have chosen to believe in an objective intelligence that is natural or scientific and beyond our limited physical existence. Or not to believe in anything. However, refusing to believe is still a form of belief, in that we have made a choice that determines how we view ourselves and our world and hence how we live life.

Awakening to our spirit means waking up to the reality of our true self in its purity. Regardless of whether we hold true to a religion or belief system, we all need to awaken if we have forgotten or deviated from our true essence. The need to awaken to an experiential reality and return to our spirit is simply a natural progression toward a higher reality in the evolution of our inner self.

To highlight our crucial need to awaken, let's look at the awareness of our souls from the wide perspective. We might be able to identify where we are in the journey of life. These descriptions and classifications are used only to convey the need to awaken our spirit. They are observations. Though these truths may appear confrontational, they are by no means critical judgments or allegations. There is a deep respect and compassion for all on their journeys. We are all at different points on those journeys. We climb our own mountains and are at different altitudes. Each mountain is different. Some are easier, others much more challenging. Climbers have different skills and experience. But at all times we have the freedom to make choices that affect our climb and to decide whether to climb. Many opt not to climb and to stay down in the swamp for a time. To help us better observe, I will deviate into the third person narrative in this section. Now let's examine several types.

Lost Souls

These souls hopelessly plunder and struggle through life, caught in the suffering and confusion of their physical existence. They rarely live but instead only exist. In Buddhism, this level of existence is termed *samsara*.

Lost souls are in this predicament either through ignorance, blindness, and the unconscious grip of fear or by choice through addiction. They are like people who live with boxes over their heads or like horses with blinkers on. They are young souls yet to evolve. They are caught up in their existence and their drama, be it traumatic or monotonous. They are not open to seeing, hearing, or searching for anything beyond their limited patterns, failing to realize that they have a choice or refusing to make one. At times they may appear almost to enjoy their suffering, since it gives them identity and attention.

They submit their power to people, events, and circumstances and are swept around by the currents of life, however mild or turbulent, getting nowhere. Life for them is like swimming upstream against heavy currents. They face one struggle after another, unaware that they themselves have created these struggles. They are susceptible to despair, depression, worries, pain, anger, rage, hate, and suffering. These souls would not be interested in picking up a book like this, and if they accidentally do, will put it away because they do not understand or agree with any of this or because some content is too confrontational. Whether by choice or through ignorance, they keep that box over their heads instead of breaking the cycle.

Their mind, body, and energy fields are rigid, contracted, blocked, and heavy. Their spirit is asleep, almost dead. These souls cannot relate to other living things, for they barely know their own living presence. They are not in tune with their bodies, emotions, and thoughts or the interconnection of life. They are prone to physical ailments, mental and emotional disorders, constant aches and pains, weak immune systems, lethargy, and premature aging.

However, this can also be the preliminary phase that may push them into spontaneous awakening, for sometimes it is only by plunging into the depths that one can be jolted into awareness or sparked with the courage to start climbing up. Many awakened souls have been spurred at this stage. All that is required is to allow an opening, even a very slight one. These souls need only remove the boxes from their heads and hear, look, and listen. Nothing will ever be the same again.

Illusory Souls

These souls generally appear confident, successful, and in control. They may have been granted fairly easy lives with few dramas, experienced loving and nurturing upbringings, and had all material, physical, and emotional needs comfortably or abundantly met through good fortune or their own hard work. Hence they may exude self-esteem, enjoy good health, and have vibrant personalities. However, their happiness is dependent upon their full sense of small self and on external objects and pursuits that have come easily for them or come according to plan. These souls seem fine, thriving with enough energy to take on the world, as long as everything in life continues to go as they plan, desire, and expect.

They submit their power to external objects or pursuits—be it a person, object, place, concept, belief, goal, dream, or identity—to feel happy and fulfilled. For some, happiness and wholeness are dependent on finding the right partner. This emotional need, dependence, and attachment carry with them expectations of love or certain behaviors in return. In the case of a goal or ambition, be it fame or financial gain, the external is again the focus; purpose and happiness are found in feeding the power of the individual. It is not wrong to have goals or dreams or to love another. But if the key to our happiness, well-being, and sense of self is in an object or pursuit, then our foundation will be unstable. Everything external, like ourselves, is impermanent and subject to change. That is the nature of this physical world. So while we should not reject people and experiences in our lives, the key is not to have attachments to them.

Illusory souls are happy when their desires and expectations are fulfilled, and they live the illusion that they can totally control and determine everything in life. They dismiss or are ignorant of the reality that life consists of more than just the limited self. It is, in fact, an interplay of other energies and events, the choices of others, and basic physical laws of nature like impermanence and polarity. The only thing constant in life is change. That is the law of the physical world. Life is dynamic, and nothing stays the same. Another aspect of the physical world is polarity: happiness versus sadness, high versus low, hot versus cold, dark versus light, and so on. Without one, there would not be the other. Illusory souls may be opinionated and obsessive. They may even be control freaks at times as their attachments feed their egos, identities, and purposes.

They may appear to have a strong sense of self, but it is only a sense of their small or limited self. They talk often about themselves, saying, "I want," "I have," "I do," "I am," "I believe," or "I know." Due to their strong attachments, their ups may be very exhilarating but their downs may depress them just as intensely. They are totally crushed and spiral into depths of despair when life does not live up to their expectations and desires. Their sense of well-being and of self may swing wildly until they find an alternative attachment to replace one that has failed. Such people can find themselves drained of energy as they go against the flow of life to pursue their strong attachments and satisfy their egos. Illusory souls face their greatest fear when they confront death or imminent death, for it is the ultimate loss of control and the dismantling of their sense of reality. Some illusory souls have glimpsed their true and greater selves beyond and within, but because of fear or the pull of attachments, are unable or unwilling to go further on the journey toward the freedom of awakening.

Awakened Souls

Human consciousness has evolved to these exciting times when many are privileged to have awakened. However, the many are still not enough. There are also many levels of awakening. Generally, these souls live with awareness and continue to learn, grow, and heal by shedding all of their physical layers. They know and have experienced their own reality beyond the limited, physical, immediate self and this world. Thus they try to trust and live with a respectful surrender to the natural flow and greater whole.

They see the interconnectedness and oneness of all of life and the unconditional love they know is their true self. They try to embrace life and live in the moment. They accept life's ups and downs with a wise understanding, seeing these things as lessons, not obstacles. Although they feel just as much as anyone else, their emotional swings are minor and less intense, since they are not attached to the fragmentation and instability of what is constantly changing. They try to live from their hearts, not their heads. Even as life's waves churn, these people remain in synchrony with the universal life force. This trust is in line with their continuous journey of release, a resolve to let go of almost all physical and material attachments without fear.

These souls live with true peace and happiness independent of anything external. They are naturally compelled to take care of their bodies, minds, and souls. As such, they tend to lead a healthy lifestyle, consume wholesome foods, and engage in a spiritual connection of some sort through meditation, prayer, creativity, communing with nature, or whatever connects with that core and silence within. They are naturally compelled to care for and help others who are suffering and do whatever good they can for the environment and mother earth, since they have a connection with all of life and recognize their oneness with all. Though awakened, they must continue to stay vigilant to avoid succumbing to the noise and pull of the physical world and the conditioning of the thinking mind.

Fully Enlightened Souls

These are few and far between. They are in this world but not of it. They exude pure spirit in a human frame. Their sense of small, limited self has given way to the universal self and wholeness. They flow with endless unconditional love and compassion. Their spirit affects others and the world around them, and they bring major changes. These souls have a vibe of peace that affects others. Their vibrations are higher than those of others and their energy overflows, so their presence alone is sufficient to change lives and awaken many. They are *bodhisattvas,* making a difference for humanity, the environment, and life. They rarely or never speak of *I* or *me*. They refrain from judging and maintain a beginner's mind with modesty, compassion, and an open heart. Although they are subject to myriad life experiences and feel joy and pain like everyone else, they are beyond the physical and material. All of life is a play and a lesson to be embraced. They flow in total synchrony with life. Some enlightened souls are widely known, while others are simply leading quiet lives.

This general categorizing of people into levels of spiritual awareness may appear static and differentiating, but it is done only in an attempt to convey the state of the human spirit through words. The reality is that life and our nature are fluid and dynamic, always open to change. The crucial point is that we have the choice to awaken, change, and flow.

Reflection

If certain words or passages in this chapter evoke feelings within you, have a closer look at your reactions. Are they objections, defensiveness, resistance, annoyance, or a quiet realization? Do you see yourself or people you know in these descriptions? Observe the thoughts attached to these reactions. Does your mind justify, disagree, agree, or acknowledge? Why does the mind have these thoughts? Where do these thoughts come from? Do these thoughts filter from your perceptions, beliefs, ideas, or opinions?

In your daily life, observe the people and the world around you. Observe your friends and families, acquaintances, and strangers, and watch the world news. Look beyond the physical and see if you can detect the spirit within each person. Then look within yourself. The need to awaken will be crystal clear as will the need to make choices toward awakening and flowing with your true living spirit.

CHAPTER 3

What Is Our Spirit?

IT IS IMPOSSIBLE TO USE words to describe a personal reality that is intangible and experiential. Words can only say what the spirit feels like and seems like and how it manifests itself. Words in this chapter may seem incomprehensible or confusing when we have not awakened. That is not a mental but an experiential difficulty. When our spirit awakens, we may read these words again with huge smiles on our faces, for they ring with truth when they are our own personal reality. This chapter will attempt to convey, through various interpretations, the experience of our pure living spirit. But to know what is spirit, we must ourselves experience it.

Spirit has no face, no identity, no name, no mind, no borders, no personality, no solidity, no noise, no beginning, no end, no place, no time. It is the stillness, the background in which everything occurs. A spirit is not an object confined to time and space. It is often conveyed and perceived as an experience. But it is an experience that emanates from the ultimate of us. Spirit-awakening experiences have been conveyed through various interpretations, each unique to itself. One such interpretation is the experience of pure spirit energy before we have allowed life to impose all of its layers upon us. Who we truly are, our pure spirit, is here and now when all that we are not is gone. Spirit is not out there somewhere, in something, someone, or some idea to be found or acquired. It is already here. We are already what we seek. When everything that we are not is let go, we are simply spirit.

When we first awaken, we may experience our pure spirit beyond our physical body as sublime peace, bliss, and unconditional love beyond words. Spirit is infinite, and the experiences, realizations, and actualizations of spirit are infinite as well. Spirit is infinite flow. Hence our experiential reality as spirit is infinite. Life force, which is living spirit, is the means by which we are manifested into form. Divine peace, love, and bliss are spirit qualities emanating from our source. We are spirit, a manifestation of our divine. Divinity is our true self. Like rays of the sun, we are part of the sun and still the sun. We are like waves in the ocean. No wave is separated from another. All waves are the ocean. Divinity is as much in us as it is in every petal of a flower and every gleam in the eye of an animal.

Through language comprehensible to the people of his time, Jesus tried to communicate the oneness of the Trinity. "God, the Holy Spirit, and I are one," he said, the Holy Spirit connoting our living energy, God our source, and Jesus representing us in human form. All three are one. The only way to freedom is through death on the cross, symbolizing the death of our form, the death of our limited self, the shedding of all the layers that make us this human person, rising again as spirit, what we truly are, into ultimate union with our source. The reality of unconditional love and oneness with all life (love one another as you love yourself) expressed throughout the life of Jesus is the awakening. Perhaps "original sin" was an idea intended to convey the inevitable *samsara* life to which we are subject once we are born and take human form. The story of Adam and Eve may have symbolized the choice of eating the "apple" of knowledge (the thinking brain) and materialism, leading to our downfall, suffering, and separation from our pure spirit. It is not easy to convey a reality that is beyond words and mental understanding, the truth of our divinity. Jesus was killed for claiming that he was at one with God, but he was the enlightened one among men.

The same essence was conveyed by the Buddha in slightly different language. The Buddha became enlightened through self-realization and taught that the key to peace and an end to suffering is within ourselves, not in anything or anyone external. He said that we alone are capable of and responsible for finding our own Buddha within. Our core is divine and all-encompassing love. The Heart Sutra teaches us to discover and realize our true self.

Emptiness and *nothingness* are words used in Eastern wisdom to convey the truth of our reality, our true self, our spirit. These words may provoke our logically dominated human brains to respond, *That is ludicrous. I can see and touch myself, so how can I be empty? And if we're all empty and nothing, why bother at all?* Logically, that would be the assumption, but experientially the emptiness or nothingness are not empty or nothing. *Emptiness* is a common translation for the Buddhist concept of Sunyata (or Shunyata) that nothing, including humans and our existence, has any ultimate substance. What we perceive as real and solid—our world and ourselves—is such only because of the perceptions through our physical senses. Our senses are limited and finite. When our bodies perish, our senses are gone, too.

The Buddha conveyed the nature of emptiness extensively in the Heart Sutra, and the ancient Chinese sage Lao Tzu presented emptiness beautifully and aptly in his prose "The Importance of What Is Not" in verse 11 of the sacred texts of *The Tao Te Ching*.

Our reality, our spirit, is a paradox because we are empty and not what we have always believed we are—solid, separate, and static. We are, in fact, everything because that emptiness or nothingness actually represents dynamic infinite possibilities. This emptiness, nothingness, or stillness revealed itself to me one day when I was practicing Zen calligraphy, writing out the Heart Sutra on rice paper with a brush while sitting on my knees for a good hour. The blankness of the paper, the characters, and the script became clear during the practice. The characters needed the blankness of the paper to take form, and the forms enhanced the blankness and highlighted the existence of the paper. We are emptiness and also form, each to realize the other.

Science has for decades been disinterested in and skeptical of spirituality and the unquantifiable or unproven, focusing only on expanding its knowledge and proofs of our physical universe. But recent times have seen a convergence of quantum physics and neuroscience with the reality of our infinite inner space. Science is now confirming what spirituality has been saying since ancient times, just with different words. Based on their studies, quantum physicists have found that what we perceive as solid matter is, in fact, just space. Quantum physicists like John Hagelin (Ph.D. in physics and consciousness) and Fred Alan Wolfe and alternative medicine expert Deepak Chopra (MD) are among those who have spoken out and written extensively on quantum theory of consciousness.

It has been said that a quantum physicist's biggest fear is measurement, because at atomic and subatomic levels, everything is just waves of nothing. Existence is merely scattered waves and becomes particles only when we try to measure, perceive, or observe. The deeper we explore apparent matter, the more the truth of existence is confirmed. If we studied a piece of wood (which we perceive as solid matter) under a microscope, then under an electron microscope down to atomic, then subatomic, nuclear, and subnuclear levels, we would find nothing solid, just space. Similarly, probing as deeply as possible into the human body, nothing solid can be found. Interestingly, the big bang theory says that life began with an explosion *of* space, not an explosion *in* space. These are exciting times as science echoes the message that all enlightened souls have been trying to convey.

What we truly are, our spirit, is that which is beyond the material and tangible. As such, it cannot be defined exactly in words. It is an experiential reality that can only be described. To know our spirit, we must experience it. This experience, called awakening, awaits all of us. Most of us may have unknowingly glimpsed our spirit already many times. The next chapter will outline how we can awaken to our spirit.

Reflection

Allow the words of this chapter to sit with you in your meditation and in moments of silence when you are alone, such as waiting at traffic lights, having a cup of tea, or lying in bed ready to retire for the night. Do not try to analyze these words with the logical brain. Even if you do not fully comprehend some or all of them, keep the words with you and remain open in your daily life. Life will reveal itself to you in most unexpected ways. Awakening may occur at any time when the realization shift occurs.

CHAPTER 4

How to Awaken

WE LIVE IN EXCITING TIMES as human consciousness has evolved in a multitude of ways to be able to awaken. In this chapter, we will learn about the background conducive to awakening and get an overview of the ways to awaken. In the next chapter, we will explore all avenues to awakening in greater detail. Several channels or one particular way may be more effective or possible than others, depending on what resonates most with the heart and soul at a certain point.

Awakening is not confined to lone mystics, monks, and sages who live in seclusion in a monastery or meditate for decades in a hidden cave in the mountains. Some awakened souls live among us, walking the streets as we do, dressing like us, holding down regular jobs, and raising families. But the awakened reflect the true nature of their spirits through their eyes, smiles, and presence. Their living presence is not confined to the raw vibration of the physical form but is the infinite, universal, and high vibrational energy that emanates from beyond.

Many wise mystics past and present have called the twenty-first century the "age of change," "the age of awakening," or "the birth of a new world age." Astrologers believe we are exiting the Age of Pisces and entering the Age of Aquarius, a time of spiritual enlightenment, transformation, and knowledge. The fact that we are reading a book like this, whether by conscious choice or propelled by something, someone, or some event in life, is a clear indication that our spirit is starting to awaken. Or we may very well already be on our awakened path toward greater growth and learning.

The first important way to awaken our dormant spirit is to choose to be open and see that which is beyond our body and mind, that which is still and quiet. We must be willing to let go of all that we think we know and all that we think we are. We cannot receive a gift if we are not open to accepting it. For some of us, reading this book may trigger a realization. For others, words in this book may be stepping-stones on the path to deeper and greater awakenings. At all times, we trust our inner knowing. If it feels right, we will trust to hear and learn, and let go of all that we are not. Once our spirit awakens, we will find that who we are is the start of an exciting journey.

The second important means to awakening is to move away from our objective mind, the logical, analytical part of the human brain. Human beings are the most advanced species on earth because of our mental intelligence. We have taken ourselves to the moon and created technology to store information on chips the size of a pinhead. However, the mental brain is also the reason for the shriveling and downfall of our spirit. Without our spirit, we will continue to decline toward empty, mechanical, superficial existence, regardless of how materially advanced we are. Once we have awakened, however, we will have the innate wisdom to use this incredible mind to its full potential to create, enjoy, and share success, happiness, and joy.

More details on the human mind are presented in chapter 8. Suffice to say that research in neuroscience, as in quantum physics, has increasingly led toward the merging of science and spirituality. Leading neuroscientists like Professor Antonio Damasio talk extensively about our conscious mind forming our reality. The mind and self are complex perceptions and connections created in the brain through the input of our senses. Furthermore, renowned biologists like Rupert Sheldrake, Ph.D., and Bruce Lipton, Ph.D., have written extensively on scientific evidence of the evolutionary mind—how the mind is not confined within the brain. The mind exists as a field and also exists within a field. The parameters of understanding the mind and brain continue to expand as technology improves and new hypothesis are formed.

This is why conventional psychology and psychiatry have their limitations. They have their place. The analysis of the mind continues to expand our understanding of thought and its connection to our body and life. The knowledge of positive thought-changing techniques is undoubtedly useful. But many patients have discovered the limitations of these disciplines. After sitting through years of psychotherapy or psychoanalysis, many have found themselves going around in circles, totally drained and getting nowhere. That is because we are using the little and limited human mind to try to solve problems created by the human mind in the first place. As extensive as the studies may seem, the reality is that they provide only limited models and procedures for the human brain. Our human spirit is infinite and cannot be reached or transcended by the brain. So the sooner we move away from the brain, the sooner and more easily we can allow our spirit to awaken.

So what are the paths and possibilities available to us on this journey toward peace, happiness, and the end of human suffering? Whether we approach it from the language of science or spirituality, some of the major channels that may lead toward awakening can be accessed through our energy pathways (*meridians* and *nadis*) and energy centers (*chakras*), since they are the means by which we are expressed in forms. Further awakenings and total realization can be reached through our energy (life force) or energy centers as they emanate from or lead to our source. Here are some of the channels:

1) Energy
2) Energy centers (chakras)
3) Meditation
4) Vibrations
5) Teachings and wisdom

Reflection

Once you have made the decision to be open for your spirit to awaken, locate your inner intuition to guide you onto a path that will lead to the realization of your true self. Trust your heart, not the analytical brain. Whenever you encounter uncertainty or confusion, sit and stay with it as you go about your life. Allow all your senses to be open—hearing, sight, smell, touch. Life will reveal itself to you; answers and clarity will come. If you remain open with a nonjudgmental mind, messages will arrive of their own accord, unexpectedly and randomly.

CHAPTER 5

Ways to Awaken

THE FIVE WAYS THAT MAY provide channels to help toward the experiential awakening of our spirit will be explored in this chapter.

1) Energy

The living energy that surges through our body and surrounds our living world is the means by which we are manifested as a physical human form. Spiritual and esoteric teachings have called energy life force or universal energy. In tai chi, qigong, Chinese martial arts, and traditional Chinese medicine, the term used is *chi*. In Japanese, it is termed *ki*, and in yogic science it is called *prana*.

Many of us who have explored and cultivated ancient internal arts like yoga, tai chi, qigong, and energy-based meditations may already have awakened to our spirits, for we may have experienced ourselves beyond the raw and physical. If this is an avenue that appeals and feels right in the heart, find a serene place and teacher who relates well and start the journey of discovery and transformation. Those of us already on our journey should stay close and be guided by our hearts. While it feels right, continue to learn, grow, and explore. When it starts to feel stale or limited, be willing to let go. Do not get attached to a teacher or the means itself or that will create a blockage. Let life take us and teach us. Be open and ready, and another means will arrive and the journey will continue. As the saying goes, "When a student is ready, a teacher will appear." Accessing the spirit via energy channels and flow will inevitably lead to working with energy centers (chakras) because they are major junctions where flows converge.

2) Energy centers (chakras)

Chakras

There are seven major energy centers (chakras) in our body. The Sanskrit word *chakra* means a "wheel or disk of energy." Chakras are vortices or centers of transformational energy, points of convergence between universal energy and our individual energy. As such, they may serve as channels or windows to our awakening. Science, interestingly, has found a correlation between the location of the chakras and major glands and nerve plexuses in the body. The depths of chakras can be explored in studies of yogic science and chakra meditations. We can awaken our spirits by working with the pure energy of chakras through sacred mantras, images, colors, and sounds relevant to each chakra. If this is an area that appeals to our soul, trust and follow it.

Working with energy and energy centers may awaken us because a soul that is lost or asleep has almost dead energy. The energy does not flow. It is contracted, blocked, and nearly nonexistent. The chakras are dormant or asleep. In those who are awakened, the blockages to pathways and centers can be detected and unblocked, leading to higher awakenings and total realization.

The energetic reality and power of chakras for healing and balancing can be extensively explored in the areas of yogic sciences. If the yogic means of directly working with the chakras does not appeal to some of us, there are other practical ways that are just as effective in accessing the chakras. In the context of this book, chakras are used only as a symbolic reference point to convey possible means toward awakening and spiritual realization. These means through the chakras are not static. They may overlap and may be used interchangeably or in correlation, all according to the flow of the individual spirit and what feels right.

Base Chakra (Muladhara)

This is our root, seat, tribal, origin, and survival chakra. Apart from working directly with this chakra through energy work, we can awaken and access it through physical experience. For example, find a means in nature that resonates with the soul. Some of us like the forests, some mountains or oceans. If we take ourselves into direct, pure experience with that life source, we will awaken that chakra. All of life, from the smallest worm to the highest mountain, exudes pure life energy. When we submerge within that energy for a significant time, our superficial layers—what we are not—will gradually peel off, revealing what we truly are.

That is the reason indigenous people of many cultures, from the Incas of the South American Andes to the Aborigines of Australia, are all deeply connected to nature, be it the mountains, the forests, the sun, or the land. Their spirit is alive because that connection with the universal life force is maintained. The spirit within us is a ray emanating from the wholeness of life. That is also why when we take away the nature—the rain forest, land, and animals—that connects with the individual spirit of these cultures, the spirit of these peoples is affected. Their connection is severed and damaged unless they can awaken to the reality of total freedom within themselves.

If we are earthy people, we can take ourselves on a pilgrimage of the soul and live in the natural environment for a time. In so doing, we will remove ourselves from the materially oriented world that creates all the noise that blinds us to our true selves.

If the forest is our connection, we could take off for a few months of camping and living there. If the mountains are our connection, we could travel there and live within them. Every day the place will reveal itself and speak to our hearts, and every day layers will be shed effortlessly, and we won't have to expend energy analyzing with our limited brains and psyches. Some of us may not have had the privilege of taking a prolonged journey for our spirit, but many of us have glimpsed this connection with the truth of our spirit when we garden (those who connect with the earth), sit or walk on the beach and watch the ocean or go out on it (those who connect with the water), watch the sunset, go for a bush walk, or climb mountains. So value those times, and make time for those activities, for they are windows to our spirit. Trust, expand, and explore, and nature will teach a great deal.

The base chakra is the root of our survival as individuals and as a species. When our life is threatened or when we come face to face with the fragility of our existence, this too may present an opportunity for awakening. We may be diagnosed with a major mental or physical disease, suffer disability, or encounter a tragedy or trauma that threatens our survival. This can strip us down to the bare core and help awaken us to our pure spirit. When we choose to be open, heal, and learn from the level of spirit, we will journey toward freedom. Confronted with the fragility of our survival, we have choices. If we choose to remain ignorant of our true spirit, we will remain fearful and be helpless victims. We will be trapped in endless cycles of pain, anguish, and despair, suffering mentally, emotionally, and physically. These cycles of suffering will project back onto ourselves or others around us. However, if we have the courage to awaken to our spirit beyond flesh, bones, and mind, we will ascend to another level of existence with true peace and unconditional love. This will be explored in chapter 14 on illnesses and imbalances.

Sacral Chakra (Svadisthana)

This chakra relates to our creativity, the natural progression toward creation of everything that builds upon our pure life. Pure sexual energy may sometimes be cited in conveying this chakra, since this is the energy of creation. Sacral chakra encompasses every aspect of creation from new life to relationships, art, beauty, and business.

Those who are naturally creative—artists, musicians, dancers, and writers—are familiar with "being in the zone." Asked how they "think" of their creations, artists in many fields will often say that their best works come from a "zone of no mind." They are lost for words because it is almost as if something totally unplanned comes from beyond and flows naturally through them when they are in the zone. This process illustrates access through the sacral chakra when our layers of limited self have dissolved on their own. We are pure spirit, and infinite possibilities flow from our universal self.

Even if we are not full-time artists, any form of creation is the channel to our spirit. By exploring and giving time to a creative endeavor that we enjoy, be it carpentry, sculpture, or cake baking, we will allow our spirit to awaken.

Many creations emanating from beyond through the sacral chakras can stimulate and awaken the spirit in others who are open, because the visual, audio, or tactile vibration of these creations resonates with relevant chakras in other beings.

Connected with the energy of creation, this chakra also pertains to relationships, especially family and intimate relationships. Our relationships with the people closest to us can unlock the deepest lessons we need to learn. They can awaken our true self if we learn and explore them. Relationships will be further discussed in chapter 11.

For some, the experience of conceiving, carrying, and giving birth to a baby, or the inability to conceive, may also awaken the spirit. New life is pure essence. Whether our own newborn or someone else's, newborn animals, or young plants, pure life can inspire in us an awakening if we will allow it, open ourselves, and be still. I experienced a profound time in my life with the birth of my first child, James. I had zero self-worth and no convincing reason for staying alive. I was still searching and asking, what is life? Then life brought me its very essence. Cradling him in my arms all night in my hospital bed, looking at his perfect little fingers, toes, nose, and mouth, soft skin, fine hair, and peacefully closed little eyelids, and feeling his soft breath, I couldn't help concluding, *Wow! If something so beautiful, perfect, and pure can emerge out of me, I must be worth something.*

Surrounding ourselves with pure living energy and beings of pure spirit gives life. It awakens that pure life within us. We should flee the buildings where we live and work, look up at the expansive skies, and breathe in the life around us.

Wealth is also part of creation. Again, lessons learned from exploring these issues may enable us to shed many layers and illusions that block this chakra, leading to the awakening of our spirit. The question of wealth will be explored in chapter 13.

Solar Plexus Chakra (Manipura)

The solar plexus chakra is the gravitational point of the energy body. Three major energy channels (ida, pingala, and sushumna nadis) converge at the solar plexus. In all Eastern forms of martial arts and internal energy arts, many skills are cultivated from this center because it is a major source of energy and power for transformation mentally and emotionally, and hence physically. This center relates to our self-esteem, sense of self in this world, and sense of true self. Exploring this area may involve finding out who we truly are through a process of self-inquiry. This process may include delving into teachings and philosophies and our personal histories or the history of humankind. Self-healing, growth, and progress toward becoming positive, thriving individuals in the physical world will lead us toward our spirit. Through learning and exploring, we can experience and discover the true self.

These first three lower chakras relate more to our primal connection to self, our base, and our relationships with the external world. Awakened, they can open the higher chakras, turning us toward our inner world and beyond on the journey of connection to our higher self. We start to live not as a limited, contracted human but as a spirit journeying through life for the evolution and growth of its pure self.

Heart Chakra (Anahata)

Awakening through this chakra initiates emotions, healing, and transformation of a deeper kind, opening us to the higher chakras of endless possibilities as we cease to live the limited human journey and start to live our spirit's journey.

This center is all about unconditional love, compassion, forgiveness, and paths of the heart. Many of us need to heal and realize unconditional love not just for all other living creatures, including those who harm us, but for ourselves. We may realize this through doing. Many who are inclined to serve others may undertake such a journey. Through selfless charity and communal humanitarian work, they may make great advances toward unconditional love. Helping and giving unconditionally awaken others as well as ourselves through the interconnection of our heart chakras. Some may realize unconditional love through parent-child or spouse relationships.

As with all chakras, a significant path to awakening this chakra of unconditional love is to let go of all that blocks the heart. Pain, anger, hatred, sadness, despair, fear, discrimination, and judgment are heavy, dense, and negative emotions that block the heart. When all this is healed and let go, all that we really are remains. We will recognize and experience our pure true nature, our spirit, unconditional love. The journey of our spirit runs through the heart. The heart is the center of emotions. We must allow ourselves to learn through the full range of emotions, honoring sadness as much as happiness, pain as much as joy, to heal old wounds and open ourselves to new paths. The greatest growth of our spirit comes through emotions of the heart.

Another major path through the heart is following our true passion in life. Passion is not of the head, but of the heart. When we live our passion, we embark on our spirit's journey, and we can't help but awaken. So in our life paths and pursuits, we must be courageous, step into the unknown, and make choices in line with our passion.

The following three higher chakras should occur only through awakening, healing, and purification of all the lower chakras. Spiritual teachings and ancient wisdom will fall into place for a fully grounded self-realization. If lower chakras are not cleared and wisdom is lacking, the spontaneous awakening of these higher chakras can lead us to lose a sense of connection with the physical world. It can lead to nihilism, arrogance, or egocentricity.

Throat Chakra (Vissudha)

This chakra has to do with our freedom to make wise choices. It involves communication of higher truth, listening with discernment and discrimination, speaking truth wisely, knowing when we are compelled to speak, when to listen, and when to be quiet.

Third Eye Chakra (Ajna)

The chakra involves our inner wisdom, intuition, and insight balanced with the ability to reason and discern with clarity in line with our true self or higher purpose. The practice of certain meditations like those of the pineal gland can lead to spontaneous awakening of this chakra, but caution should be used. As mentioned earlier, if our lower chakras are unbalanced or blocked and we lack spiritual wisdom, we risk not being grounded with balance and equanimity in living our higher truth.

The Crown Chakra (Sahasrara)

This chakra is awakened when the soul has transcended the realms of physical and human consciousness. It is said to be the ultimate union of our limited self with our universal self. The illusion is totally dissolved and one is the pure expression of the divine.

Kundalini yoga and meditation are practices that work on awakening the divine in us through the crown chakra. Once again, we risk being swept away into an expansive altered state of consciousness if we are not fully grounded and balanced in all the preceding lower chakras. For this reason, wise teachers of yoga and meditation who work on higher chakras usually use great discernment in choosing students. They refrain from teaching such practices to students who are not ready.

Some souls, however, may experience a spontaneous opening of all their higher chakras upon achieving a balance of all their lower chakras. These souls may have been here many lifetimes before and have learned and evolved to quite an advanced level for everything to unfold immediately.

The majority of souls are hovering around the three lower chakras, with maybe one or two awakened. Souls that have awakened and are on their journey are usually working upward through their chakras. Lost souls may have all chakras in slumber. Enlightened souls still walking this earth are living from the higher awakened chakras with fully grounded and balanced lower chakras.

3) Meditation

Meditation is one of the most effective and direct means toward awakening. After awakening, it continues to serve well in helping us on our spirit's journey. Meditation is a state of mind, not a ritual act. Rituals and techniques used in meditation are just means to aid in preparing a certain state of mind. Meditation can be employed to work with awakening and balance any of our chakras. As mentioned before and as chapter 8 will detail, the biggest cause of the blindness and shriveling of our spirit is our analytical mind. The logical brain is useful for the functional purposes it was intended to carry out, but it has evolved to the stage where it now controls us instead of us controlling it. In learning the art of meditation, we start to reclaim our rightful spirit and place the human mind where it should be—under our control.

Science has proved the health benefits of meditation for our minds and bodies. Neuroscientists have mapped the brain waves of yogis and monks in a meditative state and studied areas of the brain that are activated and altered. It is not uncommon now for medical doctors to prescribe meditation to help patients manage stress to improve their mental and physical health. Medical science has found stress to be a major component of all chronic diseases.

In seeking improved health and well-being, most people who have been exposed to meditation have learned the skills of relaxation, using techniques in breathing and awareness to relax the body and quiet brain chatter. This has the effect of changing brain waves from active beta waves (15 to 30 Hz) of awake, normal, alert thinking to alpha waves (9 to 14 Hz) of a relaxed, calm, creative state. The body and all its systems respond accordingly; heart rate and breathing rate slow, blood pressure decreases, adrenaline and cortisol (stress hormones) cease to be pumped into the blood, and muscles relax. The body is taken from the sympathetic nervous system of "fight or flight" to the parasympathetic nervous system. All internal organs flourish with more blood and energy, since this sustenance need not be channeled to the extremities required for "fight or flight."

Sympathetic response is crucial for our survival; this is how humans have evolved to the top of the food chain. However, the stress response is not meant to be activated continuously. Eventually, things will start to go wrong inside the body if it is in perpetual overdrive. Homeostasis (balance) can no longer be restored. The brain is the control center. All structures and functions of the body are controlled by nerve impulses that branch out from the spinal cord, hence the brain. The body does not know whether an event is actually taking place or whether we are just thinking it. When we imagine an unpleasant event, the physiological effect will be the same as if the event were really happening. When we relax the brain by quieting our thinking, the body naturally relaxes as well.

Besides offering relaxation for health of mind and body, the alpha state of meditation is the gateway to a deeper state of consciousness—the key to awakening our spirits. As the mind is the biggest hindrance to our true self, the quieting of the mind is a crucial means to allowing our awakening. Hence many Eastern teachings have evolved toward the art of training the mind. We can train to become the masters of our minds instead of being their slaves. As with a pet dog that is not trained, an untrained mind will make life chaotic, stressful, and unbearable and possibly drive us to the breaking point.

In deep meditation, our brain waves move into the theta range of 4 to 8 Hz. Mind chatter is quieted to almost nothing, our senses and all the noise and distractions they create are shut down, and we find ourselves just there, experiencing our true self. This experience is not void in the true sense of the word, but it is void of raw physical sensation. What emanates may be pure peace, bliss, or love.

Since meditation is a state of mind, it can be practiced anywhere and anytime, not just in a particular place, posture, or time. It is simply the zone where the thinking mind is subdued or trained toward a single focus. People may enter a meditative state of mind when running, swimming, dancing, playing music, painting, or doing anything else that connects with their spirit or essence. Dynamic (vinyasa) yoga practices, tai chi, qigong, and Zen walking meditation are just some of the other forms of meditation in movement. When the mind is in a quiet, still, nonthinking state, there also is our true self in spirit.

Types of meditation range from simple breath meditation (ideal for beginners) and creative visualization to colors, sounds, symbols, chi, chakra, transcendental, vippassana, tantra, and mantra to various dynamic forms mentioned before. We may find we prefer one or some more than others, since they resonate with our essence. As mentioned in the chakra sections, care should be taken with learning meditations that work on the higher chakras—the pineal gland and kundalini meditations, for example. These should be learned under the guidance of an experienced teacher. If one's lower chakras are not awakened or are totally out of balance, or if one has deep psychological issues, awakening higher centers can lead to total loss of connection with physical life.

When we have mastered the mind through regular meditation, we will find that the practice flows into our day-to-day living. We naturally become more able to tune in to our minds and bodies during life's events. We find it easy and natural to confront challenges with a calm awareness. We become more able to respond to situations rather than react to them. We become very aware of our thoughts and sensations and how they affect us. With a calmer and quieter mind, we gain effortless clarity and waste less energy on worrying. We can live more fulfilling lives, since we are more present in the moment and not constantly lost in thoughts of past or future.

A simple meditation technique for beginners is included in the back of the book. For other forms of meditation, learn from reputable books by other awakened souls or with a guide/teacher who resonates with our hearts.

4) Vibrations

Vibrations in the form of sounds, music, and colors produce energy and can affect our bodies through the chakras and our physical being through our senses. These frequencies and vibrations may aid in meditation, or they can be used practically and directly. By playing sounds on musical instruments, we can affect our spirit within. The various cultures have their own wind, string, and percussion instruments. Each sound vibrates at a certain frequency that resonates with the energy frequency of each chakra, so they are portals into our spirit. For example, drums, especially traditional tribal drums and beats, resonate with our heartbeat and our heart chakra. This can not only awaken but heal. The effort of playing the instrument releases trapped energy in that chakra and helps to rebalance. The concentration involved in playing an instrument directs the mind away from agitation and noise, quieting it. Tibetan singing bowls and gongs have long been used by monks in monasteries as they vibrate to different chakras. The chanting of sacred mantras also has a vibrational effect on our spirit. Colors are light waves at different frequencies and vibrations. Color meditations or art therapy can access our spirit through the chakras.

5) Spiritual Teachings and Wisdom

Awakening and subsequent spiritual journeys can be made on our own if we feel so inclined with the aid of books written by many awakened souls (some of which are listed under "Recommended Reading" in the back of this book) and through the Internet. Spiritual teachings of various origins are the words of awakened souls passed down since the beginning of time. They all tried to teach in language appropriate to their time. However, the information available may be overwhelming for a young soul, and discernment is required, since some teachings may be tainted by human imperfections, blinding us to the true essence. We must exercise our innate intuition and allow the inner knowing of our hearts to guide us on our journey of self-discovery and awakening.

If our soul resonates with a particular line of teaching or a particular teacher/guide, we must trust, explore, and be guided. If they exude the true essence, many who have gone before, or have gone further ahead, will be delighted to help others on their way. Our hearts will recognize those teachers and guides who maintain pureness and a genuine spirit. They cannot be identified by their physical appearance, status, titles, names, the way they dress, how much they charge, or the organizations they establish. They exude the pure essence through the way they live, the words they speak, and the look in their eyes. Genuine teachers do not have to be preordained, have impressive credentials or a large following, or regurgitate reams of sacred texts. A true teacher, guide, or friend is one who speaks the truth from the spirit straight to our hearts. Our spirit recognizes such a person. For some of us, the journey might be through one teacher or lineage of teachings; for others, it might be through a range of teachers, teachings, and avenues or through no teachers and all avenues. Each journey is unique.

Spiritual teachings and wisdom may lead to awakening and are worth cultivating. After we awaken to our spirit within, they help us mature toward higher awakenings and the ultimate perpetual union of our spirit. They serve as wise guidance toward our practical reality and our spirit's growth journey in this lifetime. However, studying spiritual teachings and conforming to rituals will not guarantee our awakening. Theoretical spiritual knowledge alone is insufficient if we do not apply it toward a direct experiential reality. As the saying goes, "Knowledge can be learned, but wisdom must be lived." To know something is quite different from living it.

Reflection

Now that you are aware of the channels, and doorways into your spirit, you can choose to access these opportunities for awakening. Instead of getting mindlessly and obsessively caught up in day-to-day struggles and the endless pursuit of the physical and material, make time for slower, quieter, and deeper pursuits. Your spirit is the quiet, unmoving background, so it is only in the stillness that awakening can occur.

PART 2

—————

After Awakening

CHAPTER 6

After Awakening, Then What?

OUR INITIAL AWAKENING MAY BE experienced spontaneously or gradually. Each experience is unique. Awakening has commonly been described as an experience of extreme peace, bliss, or unconditional love transcending any physical occurrence. Following this experience, transformation gradually begins in our lives. For some, awakening might be an earthshaking experience; for others, it might be just a subtle, quiet realization or shift. When we awaken to our spirit to that which is beyond and more than just our limited physical self, an internal shift occurs. When our consciousness expands, we move into awareness and clarity. We start to discard, change, or recreate; hence our external physical reality starts to embark onto higher paths.

Some of the signs that may naturally occur after awakening:

1) A calm seems to abide within us, leaving us less affected by petty things in life.
2) We may tend to notice those who are not awakened and the struggles that very obviously result from their choices or ignorance. We might find our circle of friends changing as we gravitate more toward like-minded souls rather than lost souls. At times those who are lost and not open may annoy us. But as we mature in spirit, our irritation naturally turns to compassion and we connect with all.
3) We naturally start to care more for our body, for others in need, and for our natural environment.
4) We may start to feel healthier because we sleep well and prefer wholesome food.
5) We start to notice the details and vividness of our lives. Sunsets might seem more beautiful than ever. We may experience awe and wonder at watching a single raindrop, feel a special warmth in hugging our children, or savor the fullness of the taste, texture, and aroma of our foods. All senses may be heightened.
6) We may tend to slow down and smell the roses and start to enjoy just being instead of always doing.
7) We may gravitate toward more exploration of spiritual wisdom, healing, teachings, and practices. We may find ourselves more in tune with our intuition.
8) Because the joy is overflowing, we may feel like sharing our profound experience with others. Or we may just enjoy basking in the overflow, staying sublimely peaceful and quiet.
9) People around us will start to notice changes in us.
10) We may find ourselves feeling happy for no reason at all.

After awakening begins the exciting journey of our spirit, our true self. We will mature our spirit through the journey of life that we have chosen, through learning and growing. The initial awakening in which we experience the realization of ourselves beyond our physical form and mind can be the most distinct and pronounced experience, since it is the first. This can lead some souls to think they have reached a kind of heaven or nirvana itself. Submerge, bathe, and soak in the experience for as long as possible. Then let it go, for it is just another experience that emanates from our ultimate self.

Many ask whether this amazing awakening experience is perpetual. The answer depends wholly on us. The truth of who we are does not change or come and go, but may appear to do so because we continually choose to drift off with what is not. After awakening, we continue on the journey of our lives, at times thinking we are unshakable until a huge wave in life appears. Unaware young souls may get swept away and lack the wisdom to transcend the illusions. We may start to feel we have "lost it." Where is that profound peace, that indescribable joy and bliss? We keep searching when all the time those things remain. But blinded by our attachments, we have insufficient wisdom to discern.

Life will hand us one challenge after another for the growth and maturity of our spirit. Trust and work with life itself. If we listen and trust that innate knowing in our hearts, life will bring events and people to help us grow. If we observe the events and people entering our lives and pay attention to our minds and emotions, we will find that everything and everyone can offer lessons toward the awakening and balancing of our chakras from the base to the crown. Brief descriptions of all symbolic references of our chakras were presented in chapter 5. If a chakra is unawakened, blocked, or unbalanced, it will impede the natural energy flow and growth toward the ultimate crown regardless of how beautiful, exhilarating, and divine our initial awakening experience was.

Each time we release a major layer of our ego self, we will feel that we have learned another personal reality, the truth in a teaching or wisdom. We may feel that we have experienced another level of awakening on our path. Such is the joy and thrill of the spiritual journey.

So after our spirit awakens, we continue on our exciting journey of peeling off and letting go of all the layers that make up our false and limited sense of self (ego self) and move toward total union and freedom with our true universal self. This journey may span many lifetimes. At every point, we have the freedom of choice. The choices we make determine our journey, hence the concept of karma. Some souls when first awakened in the present life may already seem to possess much innate wisdom. They may often be recognized as "old souls," and many of us will say, "He/she has been here before, for sure." We start on the journey in this lifetime where our soul left off in the previous lifetime. We choose to return in this present lifetime to learn more and evolve.

Our biological age is no indication of our soul's level of maturity. Some young humans are very old souls, and some older humans are very young, less evolved souls.

Whether we are a young or an old soul, after awakening the natural progression is to continue on our journey of learning, healing, and growing. Anchored in the experience and reality of our spirit, with the guidance and cultivation of wisdom and teachings, we apply, integrate, and assimilate that spiritual reality into our present lives. This now is a journey of shedding all the layers that shield our spirit until our spirit is totally revealed. One day we may find ourselves having totally vanquished all of our small, false, and limited self, by grace achieving the ultimate union with our divinity. This reality is indescribable in words.

The ultimate truth is beyond words, beyond experience, beyond emptiness or nothingness. It is total freedom. The ultimate truth of who we are cannot be defined, owned, named, or contained, since that would immediately impose upon it human parameters, creating limitation and instability. The ultimate truth is dynamic, in flux, and infinite.

People will often ask, "What happens when we get to total or ultimate realization? Are we then enlightened? Are we a Buddha? A god? Do we then have nothing else to learn? Are we then perfect?"

Enlightenment is knowing who we truly are, not as a mental concept but as an experiential reality. As a Zen saying aptly puts it, enlightenment is to see with the eye that sees us. It is here, home, where we started from, but it is also a journey in that while we are human beings in a physical world, infinite possibilities and lessons remain. Though we may still have imperfections, we are wiser and quicker to discern. We understand, transform, and transcend. We must stay vigilant to make sure we always remember who we truly are. We still have freedom of choice, and if we are clear vessels, infinite possibilities and wonders emerge through us if we choose to live in synchrony. That is the amazing beauty of the spirit's journey.

While we are spirit in human form, there will always be a journey, but the journey continues on different planes and infinite dimensions. A soul that is totally free is one that attaches to nothing, not even freedom itself. It knows that it does not know everything and that all is in infinite flux. Hence every thing and every moment are valued and honored totally as part of a greater dynamic whole. This is our gift, privilege, and purpose: to come to the realization of the nature of ourselves, then to flow with, create, and enjoy our spirit's journey and infinite possibilities through lifetimes.

The Buddha said, "There will come a time when many will no longer need words." We must all strive to go beyond words, because we can cling to words, and we should cling to nothing. The words of the Buddha are like a raft built to cross a river. When the purpose is completed, the raft must be left behind if we are to travel further. Through the Diamond Sutra, the Buddha also reminded all awakened beings to always stay alert and, "like a diamond blade, to continue cutting through the illusions of life."

This poem on the ultimate freedom of our spirit flowed through me during one of my dog walks at sunset.

Freedom

Fresh as the early morning dew
Pure as the spirit of a newborn
Every waking moment
Embellishing and bathing
in the absoluteness of freedom.

A quiet joy
Tears of bliss roll effortlessly
In the essence of connectedness
with all who have come before
and all who are here now.

The face of everyone in mine
The oneness with every blade of grass
The flight with the flocks in the sky
The dance with the clouds across endless skies
The strength with every tree
rooting deep into mother earth,
springing forth into the heavens,
extending branches of gratitude and love.

Everything falls into place.
Everything is as meant to be.
Everything continues to move in the unmovable,
Embracing allness,
Beauty in the ugly,
Peace in the turmoil,
Quiet in the noise,
Stillness in the rushing,
Rest in the pain,
Wisdom in the seeing.

The heart honors and respects,
Embraces and bows
to the natural cycle, polarity and interplay
that enrich the fabric of the whole,
One in the whole,
Whole in the one.

Colors are vivid.
Textures are defined,
Smells sharp and invoking,
Shapes accentuated.
To exist, create, manifest, experience,
And realize That in which all else arises.

Such a privilege, honor, and grace.
Such a gift and joy.

Reflection

If you have forgotten who you truly are, you must start with the crucial reality experience of awakening, the glimpse of your spirit, your true self. Growing your spirit requires feeding it every day with wisdom, teachings, and direct learning experiences. To let go of attachments to all that you are not, stay anchored in the initial reality experience, feeding your spirit through meditation or any other means enabling that connection to be maintained until you fully realize your true self. Such is your innate longing.

Wisdom and Teachings

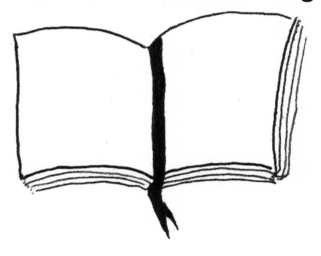

WISDOM AND TEACHINGS IMPARTED BY awakened and enlightened pure beings past and present come from the true essence itself. When we first awaken, we will already fully understand some of those words as our own personal experience and reality. Some others, however, we might hear and recognize, but not quite understand. Because the truth of our spirit is beyond the brain, they are not mental concepts, theories, or beliefs that can be understood, analyzed, forced, or faked by the mind. If we trust in our initial awakening, stay open, and are guided by our innate intuition, life itself will teach us and bring us to the realization, integration, and reality of all the teachings and wisdom. The following chapters will present teachings and wisdom in the context of major areas of our everyday lives. Some are not new to those on the path. We have heard them before, so they may serve as reminders. Others, however, may be insights that come from another perspective.

CHAPTER 7

Illusion

WHEN WE HAVE AWAKENED TO our spirit and true self, it is clear that the first distinct illusion is the perception of ourselves and our world as a solid and limited reality. Nothing solid and fixed can be detected through direct experience or science. Our external and internal worlds consist simply of space, nothingness, and probabilities. Reality is not "out there" but only seems that way based on our perception through our physical senses. Reality is, in fact, "in here." As enlightened teacher Mooji once said, "There is one earth but millions and millions of worlds." Our world, grounded in the way we perceive, interpret, understand, and interact with it, is different from another individual's world, based on our minds and levels of consciousness. Thus our reality is our own perception and creation.

The truth that there is no solidity makes clear the second illusion, that there is separation between us. If there are no clear boundaries, there is no separation or distinction. Underneath what we perceive as physical, we are all the same "soup" or matrix of nothingness. Hence we are all one. We are also one and interconnected because our physical reality is dependent upon the physical reality of other living beings and our environment. There is a natural cycle in life and interdependence among all of life. We are one with all humankind regardless of how we may appear to differ in color, features, size, shape, gender, age, personalities, attitudes, beliefs, and behaviors. Our essence and core are one and the same. External appearances differ because of geographical and natural adaptation. Our behaviors, attitudes, values, personalities, and characters differ due to the choices we have made. These are the layers we have built upon the illusion of ourselves.

We are at one with all life, from the minute amoeba to the giant blue whale. We are one with all that gives life, including our natural surroundings, the air, water, fire, sun, and wind. All manifestations of life are essentially one and connected. Our perceptions and what colors them are the cause of differences and separation. The illusion of separateness creates fear, hoarding, greed, and unhappiness as we seek to protect that separate, limited self. This illusion also causes anger, hate, intolerance, discrimination, and violence because we perceive everyone who does not recognize our small, separate self as a threat.

The third illusion is that the self and the world are limited and static. Again, direct experience after we awaken, confirmed now by science, shows that reality is infinite possibilities and that life flows from this infinite field. Thus there is no concept of time and place in reality. Everything is a continuous flow. It is our perception and attachment that create the static concept of time and place. For example, we have the illusion that life has a starting point and an ending point—birth and death—and between those two points when we experience an undesirable event, we perceive ourselves as stuck. In reality, the infinite field is not linear, and our predicament is a choice to attach ourselves to a point in the field. This illusion of limitation and linear time is a flaw in perception through a limited self. All life and the surrounding environment are a natural energy flow from the infinite field. A flow has polarities. There are ups and downs, seasons, hot and cold periods, highs and lows. To resist or interfere with the flow and cycles would impede the natural fluidity, creating a blockage or stagnation. When this condition persists and the natural flow arrives at a breaking point, it will arrange itself into a new order. When we resist the natural flow of life by seeking only what we perceive as beautiful, happy, up, bountiful, or good—and rejecting what we perceive as ugly, sad, painful, lacking, bad, down—we create suffering. The perceived external cause is not to blame.

For some souls awakened and on their spirit journey, this illusion can be well disguised and can creep in through the perception that the divine and ultimate are "out there" in some thing, some person, or some place. This perception is tempting because an awakening experience may have occurred through the aid of a particular being, situation, or place. Without sufficient vigilance and wisdom, we may erroneously attach ourselves to a belief, concept, theory, place, person, symbol, organization, or system during our journey. Who we are is not found atop a mountain, in an ashram in a faraway land, in any guru, master, or healer, in a temple, ritual, or belief system. It is right within us. If we attach ourselves to anything external as the source, we will impede the natural flow and growth of our spirit. More on letting go of attachments can be found in chapter 9.

The fourth illusion, and one of the biggest blinding us to the reality of who we truly are, is the perception that we are our mind, our thoughts, and our emotions. We are the owner of that organ in our skull called the brain, and through that we have a mind that thinks and feels, forming our perceptions, personalities, beliefs, and behavior. But we are not these things. This illusion is so pronounced that we don't even realize we are laboring under it. This is how most souls become stuck in the vicious cycle of suffering. We will further discuss the human mind in the next chapter.

The illusion that we are a solid, separate, static, limited self snowballs into the fifth and biggest illusion, that we can totally control life. We are convinced that because we are the species that has evolved to the top of the food chain and has the most advanced brain, language, and technology, we have total control of ourselves, this world, and life. The reality is that we are only a minute speck in the universe, "stardust," as someone has aptly put it. Our self, world, experiences, feelings, thoughts, and beliefs seem intense, convincing, and immediate. But this illusive limited ego self and all that it perceives, in the big scheme of things, are really nothing at all.

But when we awaken, we are life itself. Life starts to flow through us. We are in sync. We create, connect, and expand infinitely. There is clarity, peace, love, and freedom, and fear vanishes. Our life journey becomes enjoyable, exciting, and effortless.

Reflection

As you sit during quiet gaps in your hurried, everyday lives, try to recognize these illusions of our physical existence. When you are open, they will reveal themselves. When undergoing a turbulent and stressful time in life, examine the drama and suffering that you are experiencing. Look to see why you are suffering. Who is suffering? Who or what causes our suffering? Is it an event or a person, or is it your perception of an event or a person that causes the suffering?

Chapter 8

The Human Mind

We know as much about the human brain as science thus far has allowed us to understand. The brain houses our conscious and subconscious and has cognitive, analytical, and primitive functions. Humans are the most advanced species on our planet because our brain is the most evolved. The average adult male brain weighs about 1.6 kg, and until our spirit awakens, we seem to base our existence and reality upon the brain's supposed primacy. In the context of this book, the brain refers to the physical organ located within our skull, and the mind refers to the functions, attributes, behavior, and capacity of that organ. Detailed studies on the brain and its connection to the human body and behavior have been done in the fields of neuroscience and psychology.

Our brain consists of different sections that are responsible for various functions. It is the control center of the human being, directing all other organs and systems in the body. Extending into the spinal cord and linking to branches of nerves throughout the body, the brain runs the body and connects its parts. Every day thousands of thoughts stream through an individual's brain, and thousands of neurons fire and create or enforce nerve pathways. The largest part of our brain, the frontal lobes, provides for functional living, which requires processing, reasoning, problem-solving, decision-making, planning, organizing, memory, speech, and language. Stress response in the conscious or subconscious is provided by the primitive brain or limbic system (our emotional brain) in "fight or flight" for our survival.

The plight of the adult human mind is that almost all the thoughts that we produce are of the past or future; those of the present are colored by the past or future. Very rarely, if at all, are these thoughts of the pure, fresh, awakened present. We waste a lot of energy asking ourselves, *What if? Why didn't I? Why didn't she? What will happen? What may happen? Why did it happen?* We replay the past and speculate on the future. All of this is colored by emotions from the conscious or subconscious past. This often triggers a vicious cycle of thoughts evoking emotions that evoke further thoughts and emotions. Their intensity and volume keep increasing until the thinker is unable to control the thoughts at all. Thoughts start to think themselves. Thinking can be useful to human living, but excessive thinking from our limited self arises out of fear, is fragmented and futile, depletes energy, and harms the body.

The body cannot differentiate between actual and imagined events. Thinking anxious and fearful thoughts will stimulate our adrenal glands to produce adrenaline and cortisols, cause heart and breathing rates and blood pressure to increase, send blood to peripheral systems and away from internal organs, pump extra sugar into the bloodstream, and contract muscles. All these make us ready for fight or flight. Such thoughts produce a response no different from the one created by actually facing an anxious and fearful situation, such as coming face to face with a wild lion.

As mentioned in the previous chapter, one of our biggest illusions is that we are our thoughts. Thoughts occur because there is a thinker. If we can think thoughts and we are aware of them, then we are not our thoughts. We are aware that the mind thinks, perceives, analyzes, reasons, and remembers, so we are not our minds. When we awaken to who we truly are, we know that our brain and mind are just part of us, but we are not them. It has been said that consciousness is at the seat of mind.

Who we truly are is beyond brain, mind, thoughts, and emotions. The brain, mind, and thoughts are powerful; through them we can create and change our physical reality, provided we remain their master. When we are caught up in the brain's vicious cycle of futile thoughts and identify them as us, we have no control or power, and they blind us to our true self.

Buddhist spiritual teachings have always centered around training the mind through meditation. Christians pray, sing hymns, or chant the rosary. Muslims pray out loud. Hindus chant mantras and meditate. Indigenous peoples sing, dance, play music, and chant. The aim of all these practices is to center and focus the mind. If you are a beginner to meditation, use the guide at the back of this book for a simple breath meditation. The brain does not stop thinking unless we are dead, so it is impossible to stop thinking. However, by training the mind to focus—be it with our breath, an image, a sound, a prayer, a chant, a word, a name, or a dynamic movement—we train the mind to quiet down.

When we find a single, stable focus, thousands of scattered thoughts are deprived of attention and lose power and intensity. Over time, they become quieter until we almost don't notice them. Instead of a single focus, we can also use a diffused observation approach, just watching all of our thoughts but not identifying with them, attaching to them, or even resisting them. Resisting thoughts will intensify them. We must instead be neutral observers and simply deny them any attention. Thoughts will continue to feed and grow on the attention we give them. This is productive and useful if they are positive thoughts, but if they are destructive and futile thoughts, we should allow them to pass.

When the mind is trained or pacified to the point where it is so quiet that it disappears, with theta brain waves of 4 to 8 Hz, we are our true self, our spirit essence. This meditative state of mind can be achieved in a seated meditation or in a variety of other ways like watching waves rolling into shore or focusing in a yoga session. When the mind and thoughts are not there, we are simply our pure essence and spirit. This powerful theta brain wave state of mind, us in pure spirit, allows the transcendence. When we are spirit, we can heal, change thought patterns, and create. Hence we can transform our physical reality.

This blissful, meditative glimpse is accompanied by a choice. Some will dismiss the pursuit as too hard and say they can't be bothered. Others may be reluctant to let go of their addiction to compulsive thinking. Still others will persist and further train the mind. Training the mind will mature the spirit until one day all of life is a meditation. The mind then ceases to be uselessly busy and becomes precise and functional. Its functional ability and focus increase. The mind becomes as it was originally meant to be, since it is not drained of energy and fragmented in thousands of directions. Our spirit, the quiet strength and power, is at the seat of our mind.

Powerful although intangible, thoughts are essentially vibrations that can affect us, our choices, and our world. Mooji once said, "A thought without belief has no power; a thought with belief can start a war." When we are skilled at detaching from our thoughts as an observer and master, we gain more clarity and discernment. However, that requires diligence and practice because the more turbulent thoughts that seem to have power over us usually have intense emotions attached to them. Thus we need to accept our emotions, then let them go to help diffuse or eliminate them.

Emotions are part of our makeup as human beings. It is a privilege that we can experience such a range of emotions, for this adds to the richness of life. Emotions are pure energy. They become negative or positive based on the thoughts attached to them. When we face major turmoil, thoughts race through our minds twenty-four hours a day from all directions, fragmented, and with intense emotions. The intense energy of emotions produces a range of physiological effects. Apart from affecting blood pressure, breathing rates, and muscle contractions, this energy causes hormonal chemicals to be secreted into the bloodstream and surrounding cells. These can be released through crying, exercise, screaming, laughing, shouting, singing, dancing, drumming, or simply by sitting with the emotions and allowing, watching, acknowledging, and feeling them. We can go through the physical manifestations of emotions—for example, nausea, muscle pains, lethargy, headaches, and a choking feeling in affected chakra centers.

Emotions are all energy turbulence and blockages, and without thoughts they remain neutral sensations that will run their course. By separating thoughts from emotions without judgment or analysis, we allow this pure energy to be manifested, processed, and released. If they are denied or suppressed and become chronically pent up, emotions may eventually manifest themselves as chronic and serious mental or physical illnesses, irrational or violent behavior, or total breakdown. Allowing ourselves to feel and process the turbulent energy of emotions safely and objectively before they are suppressed to a breaking point is essential. We will emerge as if we had been through a storm, lighter and relieved, with emotion eliminated and the ability to see a situation simply for what it is. Often, the obvious truth of a situation will reveal itself to us.

When we are the masters of our minds and become detached and neutral observers, we will realize that without vigilance our thoughts can easily ensnare us in the past with guilt, regret, anger, and remorse or in the future with speculation, worry, anxiety, and fear. Rarely are we totally present in the moment with everything just as it is. How often do we think ten thousand thoughts while eating only to find at the end of the meal that we haven't noticed how the food tasted or what its texture, color, or smell was like?

The present is the only reality. Everything past or future resides only in the head. The choices we make in this present moment determine our future and can heal the past. We miss out so much on the beauty and joy in life if we are not here and now, but lost in thoughts. If we are fully in the present, here right this very moment, pure, fresh, and untainted, that is us in our spirit essence. The choice is ours whether to live as our pure, infinite spirit or in the limited mind.

Reflection

Start learning to be an observer of your thoughts and emotions. As soon as you can observe, you will start to detach and have more perspective, clarity, and control. If thoughts are overpowering and turbulent, find another object of focus, be it your breath, an image, a sound, or an activity. Try to divert all attention onto that object of focus, allowing existing thoughts to be where they are. After a while, see if those thoughts are still as intense and controlling. Similarly, when you are feeling happy, allow yourself to laugh, smile, and skip. When you are sad, allow yourself to cry. Notice the energy in the emotions expressed, and notice how you feel after expressing the emotions.

CHAPTER 9

Letting Go of Attachments

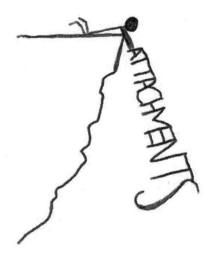

ATTACHMENTS TO ALL THAT WE are not block and sever us from our spirit. Letting go of all attachments is the key to awakening and maturing our spirit.

Attachment comes from the small-ego self. Because the small self is limited, it seeks to protect and sustain itself through power it obtains from attaching to another. Attachment is futile, since everything that makes up our physical world, everything that can be perceived and experienced, tangible or intangible, arises from the flow of existence. Hence all is subject to the natural law of impermanence, and change is inevitable. All attachment is as futile as grasping for the passing wind, a flowing stream, or a sun ray. However, human beings form attachments to their identities, personalities, roles, material possessions, pursuits, people, desires, expectations, thoughts, emotions, goals, dreams, beliefs, and concepts. Having the wisdom to be aware of attachments and the courage to let them go will restore us to our true spirit.

Letting go of attachments means releasing the hold they have on us. This does not mean that we don't care for anything. However, when we do not attach, we end up experiencing, enjoying, and loving more fully, since there is no fear of loss and thus no need to cling. Letting go requires trust and faith, but if we trust in our awakening and stay open to hear and be guided, we will make choices that are true to our hearts, not our heads, and toward the evolution of our spirit. Each time we let go of an attachment, we may almost feel like we have experienced another level of awakening, with our hearts and spirit growing stronger and wiser.

One of our strongest attachments is to our identity. This is a trait of a large majority of people, even some of us on spiritual paths. We speak and think in "I want," "I need," "I have," "I wish," "I do," "I like," "I know," and "I believe." *I* and *me* occupy a large portion of our thoughts and affect our behavior and choices. Our attachment to our small and limited self and ego is strong, even in some of us who seem very confident. We may attach to that self-image of a vibrant, attractive, self-assured, capable, in-control person. While those attributes are honorable and serve us well, if there is attachment, when one of those traits falters, we suffer.

Similarly, some of us attach to an identity of being weak, a victim, the sufferer of a mental or physical illness. When our attachment to a small, limited-ego *I* is so strong, anything that conflicts with or does not feed that identity will create separation and be perceived as a threat. When we awaken to who we truly are, our identity starts to shed its layers. Although we will still be who we are—our name, likes and dislikes, personalities, strengths, and weaknesses will remain—we will see through those layers and drop our attachment to them. We will enjoy and honor our attributes, and recognize and improve our shortcomings. But we will be open to change and growth, since we are not attached to any part of us.

Many who are suffering and ignorant have strong attachments to their pain and negativities, almost as if they are enjoying a sad, violent, angry, or depressing life story built on a web of childhood issues, trauma, regrets, blame, and repression. All we need is to be open to the truth and have the courage to let go. And why not let all these attachments go? They have not served us at all until we make them lessons to grow instead of woes to be wallowed in. By moving beyond the sad story of the past, we have the opportunity to know who we truly are.

Some have very strong attachments to their physical identities—appearance, beauty, youthfulness, strength, fitness, disabilities, imperfections. However, reality will inevitably intrude; we will grow old, may get weaker, may fall ill. Strong attachments will cause resistance to the inevitable, stifling our spirit and its grace to flow with the cycle of life.

We may also form a strong attachment to our roles, jobs, and professions. These offer immediate fulfillment, since they engage our senses in the process of doing. They satisfy our sense of small self and give us short-term purpose and a sense of achievement. We tend to fall into the trap of identifying with them. They seem to define us, but they are not the real us. We are the doers; they are just our roles. In each lifetime, our spirit chooses or is handed roles to enjoy, experience, and grow. Like everything else, they flow and change. We may progress through life in the roles of a child, sibling, student, friend, spouse, parent, worker, manager, creator, teacher, grandparent, respected senior citizen, and so on. Enjoy, fulfill, honor, and accept those roles, but let go of attachments, for these shield us from our true self.

If we aren't careful, those of us who are already on the spiritual path may attach to an identity of ourselves as a spiritual teacher, a healer, a guru, a regular meditator, a humanitarian, or an environmentalist. Although these identities are desirable, attaching to them will impede growth and subject us to instability. Although well disguised, ego and small self may creep in. Similarly, if we are not careful, attachment can occur in the awakened on the path to maturing if we attach to the beautiful experience of awakening itself or the means, technique, person, belief, or concept that helped lead us to awakening. As beautiful and divine as the experience is, we cannot hold on to it, own it, or attach ourselves to it. Attaching blocks the natural flow of energy, and our spirit will be unable to proceed on its path and may get diverted to aspects of small self like greed and ego.

For the majority of human beings today, the strongest attachment seems to be to material objects. Goods providing comfort, pleasure, and beauty are immediate and tempting to our senses. Though desirable, they should be gratefully and fully enjoyed, then let go. They do not last. Attachment to them will lead to greed, hoarding, and selfishness. Greed and hoarding are two of the major causes of suffering and inequality in the world. While the recent famine in West Africa was caused by environmental factors, the major reason people are starving and perishing is political and economic mismanagement created by corruption and greed. While many are living in poverty in underdeveloped countries and dying of famine, in the affluent West, food is thrown out as waste every night and about 80 percent of the population is obese or overweight. It does not seem like there is insufficient food to feed all of the earth's population, just an imbalance due to greed.

Attachment to our desires extends to the immaterial in the form of our expectations. We want people and life to be a certain way and expect outcomes that meet our standards and reinforce our sense of self. If others fail to measure up, we are intolerant, unaccepting, and angry. We are unable to be open and compassionate and see another perspective. This hardness blocks our true spirit.

Many of us attach to another person, be it a lover, spouse, parent, child, friend, or teacher. We often confuse love with attachment. True love has no attachments and no expectations. However, most of us love another because that person fulfills our sense of self, is our pillar of strength, makes us happy, and makes us feel whole, safe, and loved. The natural law of impermanence will subject everyone to change. The other person may leave, change in personality, get ill, be dying, or simply fail to meet our expectations over time. If we are attached, our small self falls apart.

We may also commonly attach to intangibles like thoughts, emotions, goals, dreams, ideas, and beliefs. Our biggest attachments are to our thoughts and emotions. We think thoughts and feel emotions. They make us human. They are part of us, but they are not us. We can choose, change, and control our thoughts and release our emotions safely to diffuse them. They are fluid and changeable, so to attach to them will be limiting and confining and allow us to be swept away into turbulent and obsessive cycles. We must choose to have positive, self-empowering, compassionate thoughts instead of self-defeating, egocentric, negatively conditioned ones.

As thriving human beings, we need to have dreams and goals as guides, but if we are living true to our spirit, they too may change and flow with the greater whole. As well, memories, our past, our life story thus far, make us what we are today and are part of our journey, but the journey from here on is based on our spirit awakening, our awareness, and our conscious choices. To attach to the past and all that it encompasses will create rigidity and resistance. Thoughts, beliefs, and concepts help color our physical reality, but detachment from them allows space for growth, learning, change, and possibilities.

All the layers that we have accumulated over a lifetime are attachments that the egocentric small self has embraced and that we must keep peeling off to reveal our essence. When we first awaken, some layers fall off effortlessly of their own accord. That is why we are not bothered as much by petty worries. But as our spirit journeys, we confront stronger attachments to ourselves, our illusions, our life stories, our dramas, our wants, and our aversions. The stronger our attachments, the more significant our letting go and the stronger and wiser we are revealed to be in our spirit. We feel as if we are entering higher and higher levels of awakening or expanded consciousness.

This is our journey, to awaken, to be aware, to learn and mature, by continually letting go of attachments that inevitably happen as we experience and enjoy life in our human form. We must always remember to maintain the purity of our spirit and true self. We must honor everything in life, but attach to nothing. Then we will be living and free spirits, expending less effort and enjoying more peace, unconditional happiness, and endless possibilities.

Reflection

In your daily life, start to become aware of everything and everyone making up your world. Examine your level of attachment to them. When you experience pain, suffering, turbulence, worry, or anxiety, try to locate the object of attachment causing the predicament. Then, staying quiet in your spirit, allow your innate wisdom and strength to transcend by seeing the big picture. With this insight, make the choice to let go. In letting go, you will free yourself from that predicament.

CHAPTER 10

Trust and Go with the Flow

THIS CHAPTER GOES HAND IN hand with the previous chapter on attachments and also involves the element of letting go to allow our spirit to flow. When our spirit awakens, we naturally progress toward growing innate trust and knowing. Trusting and going with the flow of life are natural when we are firmly grounded in spirit. The journey to mature our spirit involves going with the flow of life for continuous growth and learning.

The small-ego self, with its attachments, desires, limited perspective, and illusions of separation, will always battle with life and swim against the flow. Sometimes when people or events do not turn out as we desire, we may make changes if that is what our spirit is compelled to do. Going with the flow may also entail a wise acceptance of what is. There is always a higher purpose for everything that we may or may not know. It does not matter, for if we follow our hearts and intuition, life will reveal itself to us in time.

Going with the flow requires wisdom and an acceptance of life's polarities, the yin-and-yang nature of our physical reality. Because we do not live in fear with a desperate need to sustain our egocentric small self, we do not retain our attachments to pleasure and pain. We know and honor the whole fabric of life. Just as there is day and night, hot and cold, high and low, big and small, young and old, so there is pleasure and pain. We enjoy happiness, pleasure, and abundance as much as we honor sadness, pain, and lack.

In our physical world, one pole cannot exist without the other. All is a flow, a cycle, and seasons. Many things considered negative are not seen that way from all angles. When we perceive something as bad, we must ask, bad in relation to what and from what perspective? Something bad for us might be good for someone else, or something we consider bad today might prove to be the best thing for us because it led to something amazingly wonderful later. Nothing is absolute. As a Zen saying has it, "The reverse side also has a reverse side." In verse 45 of *The Tao Te Ching*, the ancient Chinese sage Lao Tzu wrote extensively and beautifully on polarities.

Going with the flow may be misperceived by the unawakened as not caring or being too passive. But to the awakened, this is not passivity, since our perception and behavior do not come from the limited boundaries of the human mind. We don't live by reacting to people and situations based on defensive and fearful conscious or subconscious thoughts and emotions. Instead we listen and trust our intuitive self. Our spirit is universal, has no limitations, knows beyond space and time, and flows with the greater whole.

When our spirit is still young, we must hear and trust the inner voice in the heart, not the thoughts in the head. When we live true to our hearts and spirit, we will know. When we make choices in line with our spirit and the flow, these decisions will feel right deep within our hearts, and we will feel at peace. Messages and assurances will come to us through people and events if we remain open to hear and see with our hearts. People and situations will orchestrate themselves into the flow, and things will fall into place. Miracles will happen, as they often do.

At times, we may struggle to hear our inner voice or almost lose trust when life confronts us with major challenges and turbulence. We must remain in the quiet and stillness, continue to trust, and remember who we truly are. This will see us through, and we will emerge with stronger hearts. Life does not hand us what our spirit is incapable of overcoming.

When we go with the flow, life becomes spontaneous and natural. Creativity and infinite possibilities flow through us, unblocked by fears and layers of illusions. Our body and mind become conduits for the universal energy to create, express, and transform.

There is an obvious analogy to mountain climbing, which I learned while connected with a Himalayan mountaineer for a time. Besides being attracted by the fame and fortune that may result, some people attempt to summit mountains to prove something to themselves and to others. Generally, they are trying to fulfill a sense of worth and purpose. They tend to take on the attitude of battle. They climb mountains to battle a giant force, and when they succeed, they claim to have "conquered" the mountain. These climbers perceive the natural life forces of mountains, such as avalanches, extreme cold and winds, low oxygen, steep terrains, ridges, and crevasses, as things to be battled. They persist in their pursuits at all costs, disrespecting other humans and the mountains themselves, hurting or destroying anything that gets in the way of their quest.

The irony is that such ego and desperation sometimes end the climber's life. The reality of the situation offers insight. The mountain is simply a mountain. It is alive because it bestows life. What appears to be a hostile environment results from natural forces such as altitude and from human interference, but the mountain has no ego intention or self. It does not seek to battle with the climber. It does not intentionally release avalanches to crush climbers it doesn't like. It does not seek to deprive climbers of oxygen, make them delirious, and hallucinate, and it does not cut their ropes. So how can anyone say that a climb is a battle to be won when a battle consists of two opposing sides intent on challenging each other?

The indigenous people of the mountains have a different relationship with their surroundings. They see themselves as one with natural forces. Nature provides them with food, water, and shelter, and these people are part of that nature. They do not seek to control but rather respect, honor, and work with nature's cycles and forces. For example, before undertaking an expedition, local climbers in the Himalayas seek the advice and blessings of a lama (a Tibetan monk) for favorable dates and times. Lamas have spent their lives studying nature's cycles, and being in tune with their higher and true selves, they can impart insightful guidance.

Before a climbing expedition, a traditional Buddhist puja ceremony is always conducted by a lama at the base of the mountain, with offerings, chants, and prayers of respect to it. The ritual is a reminder for climbers to undertake tasks and make choices with respect and honor for nature and with a deep wisdom, knowing that they are only a small part of a greater whole that is at one with them. So these climbers work with rather than battle the greater flow. Interestingly, the local people, though not equipped with the most advanced gear and gadgets and without having studied in the best mountaineering schools, end up being better and more successful climbers. They instinctively know the signs, make wise judgments, and have greater stamina and skills.

Foreign climbers will also attest to the fact that the locals who aid their climbs have an innate joy and a commitment to their unbelievably hard and challenging work that touch the hearts of many. That is because they choose to flow with life, not battle it.

We exhibit a flawed attitude in every endeavor when we are not awakened, living as separate entities with defensive egos and squaring off with each other, other species, and our natural environment. This is the attitude we adopt when events and people do not meet our expectations. Once we realize this, we must choose whether to flow or battle with life. Flowing expends less energy, since the currents take us most of the time. We move further, travel more quickly, and can laugh, take in the scenery, be at peace, and create along the way.

Life knows how to take care of us better than we do. All other forms of life, from the little earthworm to the giant Mount Everest, exist as pure life. No other life form besides human beings thinks it can control and manipulate life itself. All other life forms live in balance with nature or else they cease to exist. Cycles, seasons, adaptations, and their own little ecosystems provide for them. However, we humans want only what we prefer, and when life observes the natural cycle and won't hand us this, we resist, get irate, spiral into despair, and battle with life.

Battling, asserting, confronting, persisting, and overpowering may be perceived as strength in the limited understanding of the unawakened mind. But the awakened spirit knows wisdom lies in discerning whether a desire is part of the flow. If it isn't, we must show true strength, which means having the courage to make the right choice by our spirit. Doing this may call for us to be quiet and wait, to be accepting, understanding, and loving, to stop judging, resisting, and attaching and allow life to flow in its rightful course. The sage Lao Tzu pointed to the strength and wisdom in being as "soft and adaptable as water." Though it is soft, water is one of the most powerful elements. It can be used to cut through steel. It changes shape in whatever vessel contains it and changes molecular structure to adapt to its environment. But water always continues to flow to its destiny, the sea.

The flow of life, like the flow of a river, will inevitably encounter meanderings, whirlpools, waterfalls, and obstacles from fallen debris. This is only natural. But these things are all part of the river, and the flow will restore and sustain itself and continue. The awakened spirit's journey toward self-realization can be summed up as continually letting go by trusting and flowing with life. Our journey consists of existing, enjoying, experiencing, learning, growing, creating, keeping vigilant and aware, and letting go of all that is not true to our spirit. We gain total freedom when we hold nothing. Paradoxically, because we hold nothing, everything is experienced and enjoyed in full purity for what it is at the moment.

Reflection

Take notice when you encounter resistance, a dilemma, or a battle. With an awakened spirit, hence a wise inner knowing, and the bigger picture in mind, look within yourself. What is the reason for the resistance or the battle? Does it have roots in the ego? Do you resist and battle because an event or person threatens your sense of small self, your ideas, beliefs, or expectations?

If you choose to continue resisting or battling to define and sustain your limited sense of self and all it upholds, you will be battling on your own. Be prepared to expend all your energies and move toward an outcome that may or may not be what you desire. But if you choose to stay true to your spirit, you will be instinctively compelled to maintain the flow of life and see the bigger picture. Flowing with life will result in the right actions or nonactions, words, and decisions. You will be confident, at ease, and at peace and will decide and act accordingly. And life will work with you.

CHAPTER 11

Unconditional Love

OUR HEART CHAKRA, ONE OF the most significant and crucial centers for awakening, healing, and balancing, is also one of the most direct routes to transcendence of our spirit. Unconditional love is the emanation of our true self, our essence, spirit, and divinity. It has the power to transmute, transform, and transcend. Pure life, the way in which we entered this physical world, is pure, unconditional love. When we awaken, this becomes our experience and personal reality. The Persian mystic Jalaluddin Rumi wrote extensive and wondrous poems on the reality of our spirit of unconditional love.

Unconditional love is all-encompassing and without attachments, conditions, or judgment. It is distinctly different from egocentric self-love, which is centered around the ideas, beliefs, values, opinions, attitudes, conditions, and judgments of our limited self with all of its illusions. Unconditional love is also not romantic love, since almost all romantic love involves attachments through needs and desires, hence conditions.

We can learn about unconditional love by cultivating the teachings of the Dalai Lama, the Buddha, Jesus, and many others who teach and embody it and can help us toward self-realization and enlightenment. We can follow and practice spiritual teachings diligently until they become us, or we can let go of everything that is not us—our false self with all its layers—and lo and behold, we are simply unconditional love.

The uncovering of unconditional love begins with the self. We can't love another when we don't know who we truly are. Unconditional love for others goes hand in hand with unconditional love for ourselves. Unconditional love for self is not egocentric love, self-confidence, self-esteem, self-worth, pride, or arrogance. Self-confidence, self-worth, and self-esteem flow from unconditional love. We don't have to make ourselves confident, worthwhile, or self-loving. We must simply work on finding out who we truly are, then always remember that. Once we have realized our true self beyond the mind and body, awakening our spirit and living as spirit, we are unconditional love. All else flows from it.

To love those who love us and are good to us is easy. To love those who are indifferent to us is workable, but to love those who have harmed us, intentionally or not, is true growth and realization. It is almost impossible in some cases to force ourselves to love those who persecute, wrong, or hurt us and those with whom we are in conflict. But when our spirit awakens, we discover and experience the reality that we are all the same and one essence—unconditional love, peace, and divinity. It is our attachments to illusions, desires, and a false sense of self that make us into varied characters. His Holiness the Dalai Lama embodies the spirit of unconditional love in its purest form by maintaining compassion and holding peace for the Chinese despite their invasion of his land of Tibet and denial of his people's freedom.

If what others do or say triggers a negative reaction and stress in us, we must remember that these souls are merely mirrors that reflect layers of our own limited self that we need to jettison. If we let go of all that we are not, all our layers, we are our true self and spirit, peace, wholeness, and unconditional love. What others do and say will not cause turmoil. We may still feel the sensations of hurt, pain, or annoyance. But as easily as we feel them, we will see with compassion what lies beneath human layers. If anything can be said or done to help or change the other, we will be compelled to do so through the wisdom of our hearts. If not, our hearts will know and respect the truth that all of us have our own journeys and choices in life.

The heart chakra is the center of emotions. If our hearts have been hurt or broken, whether in childhood, our upbringing, or our relationships, we must heal. The key to awakening our spirit and maturing through the heart chakra is through a journey of emotional healing. Everything in life happens for a reason, and we must trust and flow with it. The greatest growth of our spirit comes through the heart, through laughter and joy as much as tears and pain. Healing involves facing, allowing, accepting and processing all those emotions, then forgiving and letting go.

Many experiences make their mark on our bodies. Memories are stored in our cells biochemically. Blockages are created in our energy flows. Neural pathways are created in the brain through thought patterns and conditioning. When our spirit is awakened, the journey to heal our hearts begins—a journey of transformation that can lead to full awakening and total realization of our true self. When we choose to let go of all, shedding attachments to hurt, hatred, anger, sadness, grief, pride, arrogance, rigidity, and resistance, we are unconditional love, peace, and wholeness in its purest form. We exist for all and for self, since all is self and self is all.

The journey to heal our hearts and move toward our true self, unconditional love, involves allowing all emotions to be experienced rather than suppressed and denied and then letting go with understanding and compassion. As explained in chapter 8, if we suppress the energy of emotional turbulence, it will take its course internally. It will lead to a vicious cycle of turmoil, despair, and confusion and eventually harm our bodies and minds through our natural physical survival mechanism. Thoughts must be restructured and reprogrammed, new neural pathways created, and old ones defused. We must build wise and empowering thought patterns to support the processing of our emotions as we allow, experience, release, and transmute them.

This can be done by choosing to break out of patterns that do not serve us. The choice to be open, learn, grow, and change requires courage. It is easier to choose to remain stuck in a vicious cycle of identifying with all that we are not, addicted to our dramas and sufferings and blaming others instead of taking the responsibility to change. We must have the courage to take a step into the unknown, out of our comfort zone, letting go of all that we think we know. Forgiveness, understanding, compassion, and trust are components of the heart.

Some blockages to our hearts involve imbalances on the other end of the scale. We may have grown up with a strong sense of self and rigid beliefs and opinions centered around the limited self. We may uphold these beliefs and opinions with an air of arrogance and a "holier than thou" attitude. We judge, resist, and reject anything that does not conform to our values and beliefs. We try to control and manipulate people and situations to fulfill our small sense of self. In the same way, we impose high and rigid expectations on ourselves. To realize this and let go of all these layers will free our spirit and its essence of unconditional love.

Healing and improvement of the mind and body through our heart chakra should be done in line with our spirit in order to gain wisdom, clarity, and transcendence. Thus it is crucial to first awaken our spirit, then stay true and trust in that which is innate in us. Healing and growth involve integration of all aspects of mind, body, and spirit. The next chapter will delve into relationships that flow out of our heart chakra. Unconditional love gives rise to the fulfilling and rewarding gift of relationships and connections with each other.

Reflection

In your meditation and quiet times, reflect on the nature of unconditional love. Look within yourself and those around you, and be aware of the times when you have experienced unconditional love. Notice the difference between unconditional love and conditional love.

CHAPTER 12

Relationships

IN THIS CHAPTER, WE WILL take a closer look at the nature of the major relationships in our lives in the context of wisdom derived from awakening. We might gain insights into our relationships and how we can apply our spiritual reality to honor our spirit's journey.

As human beings, we have the gift of being able to love, nurture, share, support, grow, and learn from each other through relationships. All relationships have their place, and unconditional-love relationships, whether between parent and child, teacher and student, siblings, lovers, spouses, friends, or total strangers, add to the richness of our lives and nurture our hearts and spirits.

Parent-child and spouse/partner relationships, however, play the biggest roles in matters of the heart. These relationships can touch areas in us that no other relationships can and offer healing, growth, and learning. Our spirits have chosen the people in our lives, especially those in the most significant relationships, so that we can evolve toward our ultimate realization.

Parent-Child Relationship

Some of our biggest issues in life stem from parent-child relationships, our childhood, and upbringing. Our parents or primary caregivers are the people through whom we learn about love and our physical world. With their love and support, they helped mold us into what we are today. We adopt views, attitudes, beliefs, and ideas and develop personalities and characteristics through the experiences of our childhood. Those who experienced trauma and pain rather than love and support were molded accordingly.

Almost all children will have issues with their parents, their past, and their upbringing. Almost all parents did the best they knew how to do. The reality is that our spirit has chosen particular souls as our parents to present lessons we must learn in this lifetime for our growth and evolution. So the sooner we let go of whatever issues we have with them, the sooner our spirit can be freed and allowed to flow.

No relationship teaches a greater lesson in unconditional love than the parent-child relationship. In an ideal world, all parents would love their children unconditionally and vice versa, but unless we are awakened to our spirit, many of us will project our desires, expectations, issues, and layers onto each other to fulfill our sense of small self. Letting go includes healing. This means processing all attached thoughts and emotions in the light of our spirit with wisdom, understanding, and clarity toward peaceful acceptance, forgiveness, and unconditional love.

Issues with our parents and our upbringing are at the root of many persistent attachments and our autopilot reactions to events and people in our day-to-day functioning. These hurts must be healed and released. If not, they will hinder our present and affect our future through the restricted and limited actions of our present. Life has a way of continually spotlighting these issues until we learn, since our spirit has the innate longing to awaken and flow. So we will find ourselves in repeated scenarios, confronting the same root issues again and again in this lifetime and many more ahead if we choose to stay ignorant.

Whether our parents have the wisdom to change, learn, and grow from their relationships with us is their choice. If life compels us to do or say anything toward the growth and change of their hearts, we may do so unconditionally, but we must attend to ourselves, restoring the garden in our own backyard first. Then, if it is meant to be, life will compel us to help our parents fix up their backyard. If they choose to reject our help and don't want the yard fixed, we must respect the fact that it is their yard and their choice. Our parents have chosen us as their children to learn crucial lessons in this lifetime, and they too have their own journeys and choices.

Often when we are awakened and exude pure spirit, our unspoken peace and unconditional love may touch and awaken the slumbering spirit in our parents. Sometimes life has its own way of working things out through the power of doing less or doing nothing at all. When we awaken and live as spirit, unconditional love is what we are. We find ourselves loving our parents simply because we do, not because we ought to, not because we don't want to lose an inheritance, not because we feel sorry for them, not because they might change, have changed, or won't change, and irrespective of whether they love us in return.

On the other side of the coin, we who are parents should realize that our spirits have chosen particular souls as our children to offer certain profound lessons and realizations. Often it is only when we have become parents ourselves that we gain compassion for our parents' shortcomings and faults. A major flaw in the human mind concerning the parent-child relationship is that a parent is superior and knows all. Some parents are younger souls than their children. Their spirits are here to learn much from their children. This is not to say that as parents we should not exercise responsibility, provide discipline, and have confidence. We are, in terms of physical existence, more experienced than our children. It is our role to bring them up safely in this physical world, ensuring that they are well equipped mentally, emotionally, physically, and spiritually. However, significant as this role is, we must honor it with a quiet knowing and respect, realizing that as much as we are a gift to them, they are a gift to us as well.

Our children do not belong to us, as much as we love them. They are souls to themselves. They have their journeys just as we do, and must grow and learn lessons in life. It has been said that our children are only lent to us for a short time, that we don't own them. We sometimes feel pain as our children grow older and leave or make choices that we see as detrimental to their spirit. However, we must respect their need to live and learn through their own journeys. There is no greater gift we can give than just being there for them with unconditional love. As much as we claim we are doing it out of love, to conform them to our needs or our plans for how they should live will restrict the flow of their spirit. Unconditional love does not seek to control, possess, manipulate, or restrict another for the satisfaction of our own values, beliefs, standards, expectations, needs, and desires. These are based on our layers of fear and illusion disguised as love from the limited and small self.

Courage, strength, and growth are not possible for our children if we shield them. We learn and evolve most through our biggest challenges, pains, and tribulations, so we must accept that such difficulties will be part of their journeys in life. We learn from our mistakes, and our children must be allowed to make them. The spirit grows not in completely avoiding mistakes, but in knowing we have made them and choosing to learn from them.

We must always be open to our children in mind and spirit, and we must not be quick to judge, for at times they may teach us a great deal if their souls are more advanced than ours. If we stop to listen and see from another perspective, we may be amazed at what we can learn. Toddlers and very young children, for example, can teach us a lot when they stop to smell the roses or when they express themselves with innocence and fullness by crying and screaming at the top of their lungs, laughing, and giggling. The unconditional love and pure energy they radiate touch that same essence in us, which is also us, but which we often choose to forget. If we parent with unconditional love, open hearts, and our inner wisdom as a guide, we will enjoy each precious moment with our children, delighting in the ups and downs of life with all its excitement.

When we are awakened parents, our gift is to love our children unconditionally, even if they misbehave, make choices not in line with ours, have imperfections, and fail to love us in return. We still parent firmly. We may guide, discipline, and reprimand, but our love is not given or denied based on conditions. Our role as awakened parents is to support and maintain our children's true spirit, their pure essence from birth. As they progress on the journey of life, the inevitable process of adding layers continues through the education system, community and social life, career, marriage, material pursuits, and later parenting themselves. Through our close and unique relationships with them, we can try to maintain their connection to the spirit, always helping them through the things we do and say to remember who they truly are, thus keeping their spirit alive and as free as possible. If our own awakening has occurred only after our children have grown and "lost" their spirit, we still have an opportunity to help them toward their awakening.

For many, this role may also be played in a special way through grandparenting. Besides being able to impart to grandchildren the wisdom of life and spirit, grandparents have the privilege of more time to be their pure selves rather than rushing and doing, and this is a gift for both them and their grandchildren. With time spent together, grandchildren often instill more life and vigor into grandparents through their younger energies.

Romantic Love Relationship

Among the most frequently asked questions are: What is true love? Is there such a thing as true love? Why is there always a quest for true love?

Yes, there is true love. It is unconditional love, our true self. Hence the quest is futile. True love is not found in another person. It is here now within and is us in our pure selves when all that is not is let go. When we know who we truly are, we are unconditional love itself and complete. There is no lack, need, or desire requiring fulfillment by another. The love we have for others is just an overflow of our wholeness. Again, this is not just an ideal but a personal reality that is us when we experience the realization of our true self.

True love can exist between two people, though it is quite rare. Most romantic love between two people who are termed "in love" is really just attachment. When we are young or of child-bearing age, we are propelled by nature toward physical attraction for another to serve life's significant purpose of reproduction. At the same time, our spirit tends to attract another and vice versa in line with its purpose and longing for awakening, growth, and learning. Our spirit continues on this innate path throughout life in subsequent intimate relationships if we end up moving on from one to another. This is because the people most intimate to our hearts have the potential to reach areas and issues deep within us that other people do not. Our greatest joys and pains may come from these relationships, but so do our greatest growth and learning in spirit.

If we study closely the nature of almost every romantic relationship, we will detect needs, desires, demands, and expectations. But true love does not need, demand, expect, or possess. It is simply the sharing of an overflow. In most partner relationships, there is a transaction of demands and expectations. We often hear people say, "He does not give me this," "She is not like that," "I want this," or "I need that." We love another because that person provides us security, comfort, self-esteem, happiness, fun, and physical gratification. We may deep down love another simply because he/she is a perfect parent for our children, or a good wife or husband, or we may love someone because that person loves us. This still is a condition. True love loves another even if the love is not reciprocated.

As long as love is based on needs, desires, demands, and expectations of the small and limited self, we will continue to feel lack, search, or move from one to another, and not find true love. For a few months or years, we might perceive the other as fulfilling our needs, but life is a flow and we change, the other changes, and our needs, desires, and expectations change. Unless we, the other, and all of life flow in connection, there will come a time when we say, "I am not in love anymore" or "He has changed." We are always changing, and so is everything around us. However obvious or subtle, that is the nature of all things.

If our so-called love is dependent and attached to another, it is subject to change and instability. That is evident in the rising rates of separation, divorce, and multiple partners. We change partners as easily as we change cars, and as in the case of a new car, the novelty of the new relationship is always ecstatic and sublime. But if our lack within is still the basis for the relationship, then after the novelty wears off, we will eventually repeat the same pattern with the same issues, just with a different partner in a different scenario. If our relationships are based on lack in our limited self, then in the initial novelty phase, our perception will always be flawed. We see in the other what we want to see, and the other, consciously or unconsciously, tends to project to us what we wish to see. Our true selves and our layers reveal themselves slowly as we share our lives.

Sometimes two people may end up journeying together for the good of both their spirits. They might be termed soul mates. If their connections are maintained throughout their learning and growth with each other, they journey together toward dissolving their limited selves, maturing into their true selves, and emerging into unconditional love. This ideal does exist.

Also possible is the joining of two awakened souls who come from wholeness and so do not seek the other for fulfillment of their lack and needs. Their unconditional love for each other does not produce a relationship of needs, desires, and expectations but of giving and receiving. Work is required on both sides to maintain balance and mental, emotional, physical, and spiritual connections. Theirs is a relationship of giving and receiving, and mutual learning and growing. Generally their partnership is flowing even if they may encounter hiccups along the way. The two are connected in spirit and so are deeply in tune. Such a true love relationship is most rewarding and a great gift.

All relationships, including friendships, business partnerships, parent-child relationships, and, most significantly, intimate love relationships, are works in progress. All relationships, like all people, are part of a flow. Relationship is not a noun, but a verb.

Oneness Relationship

When we are awakened, our unconditional love is naturally all-encompassing, for true love has no boundaries. The pure essence in us is the one in every life around us whether it is another human being, a tree, a cloud, a mushroom, a snail, a lion, a sunflower plant, a noxious weed, a white man, a yellow woman, a black boy, or someone who is fat, impoverished, less educated, primitive, physically disabled, young, old, big, or small. It is attachments and choices that make one person different from another. The pure essence of life in Mother Teresa is the same in a murderer. The difference is in the choices each has made. One has chosen to be true to her spirit, and the other has chosen not to know his spirit but attach to the identity of separation, hence fear, threat, heartlessness, insensitivity, callousness, anger, vengeance, and many layers of warped dysfunction. But the all-encompassing love of an awakened spirit naturally extends compassion to all souls. In compassion, we are pained by the suffering, ignorance, and blindness that result from people's choices to deaden their spirit, but we connect with the untainted pure essence in them, hoping that someday, somehow, in some lifetime, they may awaken and grow. We may not like what they have chosen to become and how they have chosen to behave, but we have compassion, for we know what they truly are, even if they don't yet know themselves.

Reflection

Examine the nature of all relationships in your life with your awakened spirit and the clear insights it offers. Allow the true nature of those relationships to reveal itself, and then nurture relationships of true love and compassion, stemming from our core spirit of unconditional love.

CHAPTER 13

Health

WHEN WE AWAKEN TO OUR spirit, we naturally care for our bodies, and as spiritual writings contend, our bodies become temples of the holy spirit. Not far from the truth at all, this becomes our reality. It is a gift to have a healthy body and a productive life and a privilege to manifest in physical form to experience and enjoy life. We must play our role in maintaining this vessel. This chapter will outline current attitudes toward physical health. The next will present some insights into the nature of illnesses and imbalances. Please note that points conveyed in these two chapters do not constitute specific advice or treatment recommendations. We should always consult our health care practitioner or physician for properly supervised treatments.

Good health is all about balance. It is about the integration of many levels of our being, not just the physical. But the three most obvious and significant are the mind, body, and spirit. The human body is not just flesh and bones, but also a brain and mind that control the body. The spirit is the living essence or life force in the body. Attending to one aspect without the others is limiting and creates instability. When we awaken, we naturally flow toward aligning the mind and body with our living spirit.

Awakened spirits are in tune with their bodies, and if we listen the body will work with us toward optimum functioning. The human body is an ingenious living machine. From the most minute cell to its myriad processes and systems, the body has an intelligence of its own, and its components interrelate and function together in perfect balance under ideal conditions of homeostasis. Our pace of life, our environment, the foods we eat, and external and internal stress create strain and may upset homeostasis, but if we listen to our bodies, we can always correct problems before the balance tips.

Concerning health, as with everything else, if we work from the level of our spirit, processes flow more naturally than if we work from the physical limited self. Working from the raw physical level without the wisdom of our spirit, we may start off intending to do the right thing but get caught up in our attachments and illusions. For example, many active people have tipped the balance. Sports and exercise are good for our bodies. Without a wisdom grounded in the spirit, however, many have gone overboard and become obsessed with the feel-good adrenaline, image of health and the body beautiful, and the identity and confidence this attachment creates for them. A healthy activity like a sport then gets taken to the extreme and becomes harmful. The body is pushed over the edge, suffering from lack of recovery, lack of stretch management, harsh diets, artificial and chemical supplements, and insufficient rest. The body undergoes stress, weakening the immune system, increasing the risk of injury, and worse, leaving long-term damage to internal organs and systems.

However, if we are grounded in the spirit and are still driven to such extremes, perhaps life has a greater plan, as with some elite athletes. If such high-level sport is the passion of their hearts, not an egocentric pursuit, this is their path to honor and enjoy. But those of us who push our bodies beyond their limits for reasons of fear, ego, or pride, aiming to define our small self, should perhaps take a journey of self-discovery first.

I have worked as a remedial massage therapist in the natural health care industry for over a decade, and the poor choices that the majority of human beings make in managing their health are very obvious. We seem to choose ignorance or denial, then place the responsibility for our health in others' hands. The common mentality is that the body is invincible, and if and when it breaks down, there will be a quick fix. The common preference is to mask symptoms so that we don't have to attend to the causes of physical imbalances.

In the area of musculature, I have seen shocking cases of frozen muscles, or what science terms overfacilitated muscles. Clients have collapsed from whole-body muscle spasms, have been rushed to the hospital by ambulance, and a few days later have been referred by a doctor to my treatment table because their muscles have a mind of their own. Massage or any form of soft-tissue manipulation is limited because they are in such intense pain. Their tissues are rock hard like a piece of frozen steak. With such congested tissues, it is no wonder they have collapsed; water, blood, lymph, and nerve impulses would all have shut down.

The body is a living thing. Muscles need water to hydrate. Blood transports oxygen and nutrients, lymph forms part of our immune system, and nerve impulses activate muscles and need water to transmit. If muscles are starved to such a state, imagine the condition of our cells, internal organs, and brain and how this affects the body's functions. We all know that the mind and body are connected. It has become obvious in the course of my work that the state of the body reflects the person's state of mind and lifestyle. In general, type-A personalities, who do not know the concept of time out, constant worriers, and pessimists carry heavy blocked energy and physical imbalances in all their tissues. I have often encountered clients who have perpetual tension and contraction in their musculature due to mental and emotional hang-ups. Even superior muscle manipulation techniques that I have used to release tightness in an Olympic athlete's musculature fail to improve the musculature of these clients.

Many of us hold on to destructive mental and emotional patterns and refuse to take responsibility for changing our lifestyles. We remain stuck, and this is reflected in our bodies. A hardened mind will naturally result in a hardened body. We pay more attention to our cars and material goods, getting them serviced and polished, than we do to our bodies. Material goods can be replaced, but the human body is irreplaceable. When we are well, we do not value and appreciate our health. Only when we lose something do some of us try to redeem it.

If we choose ignorance, our spirit will remain unawakened, our minds will be cluttered and congested, our energies will be depleted, and all our physical parts will be out of sync with each other. If we choose to realize, this will change. When we awaken our spirit, the flow can start.

The natural law requiring balance for health extends into the area of rest versus play. Sufficient sleep and down time are required to allow recovery, rejuvenation, and consolidation. Sleep produces melatonin, an essential hormone that protects nuclear and mitochondrial DNA. Rest should naturally follow play and work. However, the quality of rest these days is an issue. Many who are chronically stressed physically or mentally may be caught up in the stress cycle and are unable to escape it. Therapies and arts like meditation, yoga, tai chi, and massage may help break the cycle, but ultimately we must choose to be free of it. When we awaken to our spirit, it is only natural that we slow down. Spirit is quiet and still. It is in the quiet—in being, not doing—here and fully in the moment that we experience and are spirit. We naturally make time and put in the effort for that stillness in our busy schedules.

The choice to consume more water is a natural progression of our spirit toward better health and greater vitality. The human body is about 70 percent water, and recent science has made astounding discoveries on the adaptability and powerful nature of water. (See the BBC documentary *Water: The Great Mystery* on YouTube.) Science has found that water can change molecular structures based on its surrounding environment. In other words, water is a living substance with memory. Apart from the obvious benefits of water for our skin and elimination systems, every cell and process in the body requires some kind of element from water to function. Consuming at least six to eight glasses of water per day is essential. If we wait until we experience the thirst sensation, the body is already dehydrated on the intracellular level.

Likewise, good food is desirable for a healthy body. When our spirit is awakened, we naturally gravitate toward wholesome foods, as they make us feel energized and fulfilled. We tend to steer away from non-nutritional and energetically depleted processed foods and substances, which harm our bodies and block our spirit. Whether we decide on a vegetarian or vegan diet or one that includes meat is a personal choice. The food industry is driven by media, advertising, and vast profit margins. We need to research and inform ourselves, listen to our intuition, and strike a balance that feels right for us.

In developing and poverty-stricken countries, there are limited or no choices of food. That there is food and water at all is a gift. If our spirit compels us to eat less or no meat for the betterment of the environment and other living beings, then it is effortless for us to do so and we undertake this change without a huge fanfare. If something feels right deep within us, we simply follow that prompting.

Regardless of our choice of diet, we must ensure that we eat foods respectfully and with gratitude, consuming only what we need. This involves keeping ourselves educated on how and where our foods are obtained and on their quality. Foods are not just boxes in the supermarket fridge or cans on a shelf. Apart from their obvious nutrition, fresh foods are living things that contain life force, energy from nature and the environment—from sunlight to fresh air—that they soaked in to grow and ripen. The freshness and mode of cultivation affect foods' wholesomeness and vibrations. Foods mass-produced using chemicals, artificial means, or modifications are depleted of nutrition and will infuse our cells with toxins and impurities. In choosing sustenance for our living being, it is wise to ensure feeding our physical cells with nutrition and rejuvenating our living spirit with pure life force.

The ethical nature of foods also affects their vibrations and quality. It requires little effort to keep ourselves informed on where and how foods are sourced. If foods come from companies that through ignorance or greed abuse, exploit, and deplete other humans, animals, or our environment—other living beings in the cycle of life—we may choose not to consume these unethical products. Apart from the obvious moral and ethical aspects, foods obtained by causing suffering to another are depleted of life force and nutrition. For example, eggs or meats that are obtained through unethical and intensive commercial farming will naturally harbor stress chemicals and hormones released by these animals into their flesh and blood. Our reality as a living spirit is at one with all other life. Our spirit may compel us to pay an extra dollar for fair-trade coffee or free-range eggs—simple yet powerful choices.

We must take care that whatever choices we make are not rooted in the need to create an identity for ourselves, in a cause that we are using to define ourselves, or in a deep-seated emotional or mental blockage that creates a dependent relationship with the foods. Life has a way of maintaining the big picture and working out its own balance. When the balance is tipped, nature knows how to readjust and shift itself back into balance. We must do our part by making choices that align with our spirit and respect the interconnectedness of all life.

If we make choices based on attachments, though pure in intent initially, they will disrupt the natural flow of the big picture and subject us to instability. For when there is attachment, greed and abuse may eventually enter in. This is evident in the plight of the South American and Asian rain forests. Large expanses have been cleared for soy plantations serving bio-fuel companies and for hydro and alternative energy projects. Human logic and sense can be blinded by economics and greed. That is why it is essential that we stay true to our spirit in all areas.

Finally, let us refer back to the importance of sustaining health through the integration of all aspects of ourselves, not just the physical, but also the mental, emotional, and spiritual. All these must be in balance. The good news is that when our spirit awakens, this spiritual health naturally filters through to our lower levels of existence. An awakened spirit is naturally vigilant about mental and emotional housekeeping. With our spirit wisdom, our awareness is sharp, and we direct our thought patterns toward desirable, empowering, compassionate, and positive images, knowing that our thoughts have the power to create our realities and affect our bodies. We dismiss self-defeating, judgmental, depressing, and futile thinking, which sends neuropeptides and cortisols into our internal systems.

Compassion and love are us and flood through our system as seratonins and endorphins. Similarly, the healing of old wounds reverses the toxic buildup of harmful, pent-up emotions. With our spirit wisdom, these are transmuted and dissolved. We would not keep old, rotting foods in our refrigerator, so why would we keep old, rotting emotions in our bodies? With less baggage, we are lighter and cleaner. With fewer blockages, our energies flow more efficiently and we are less consumed by futile thinking and doing. We allow the free flowing of our spirit toward vitality, peace, and happiness.

Therapies like hypnosis, emotional freedom technique, psychology, psychotherapy, counseling, and neuro linguistic programming may be employed if we are inclined toward any of them and they feel right within our spirit. They can aid in thought restructuring. Reiki, chi healing, pranic healing, and other forms of energy healing may help mend emotional wounds and release energy blockages. Kinesiology may help heal mind, body, and spirit. Meditation can give us the ability to self-heal. Meditation allows us to be directly in spirit, providing innate wisdom and guidance in the release and transmuting of emotions and restructuring of thought patterns in theta brain waves.

To reiterate, good health, like everything else in life, is all about balance. The physical human being has limited ability and capacity, and so working with and listening to our bodies will see us in good stead for the long haul. Our being is not just that cadaver in the lab. Surging with life, it is a living, thinking, feeling union of mind, body, and spirit, and all components go toward sustaining the balance of a healthy and efficiently functioning vessel.

Reflection

Review your life and choices made toward your health of mind, body, and spirit. Listen to the innate knowing of your awakened spirit, and you will have the courage to make choices toward change, growth, and learning. In maintaining and nurturing your physical vessel through all its connected levels, immense joy will return to you as you reap the benefits of a thriving being with energy, health, and fulfillment.

CHAPTER 14

Illnesses and Imbalances

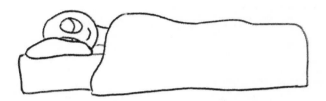

ILLNESSES AND IMBALANCES ARE COMMON in life. Most of us have been ill or out of balance or know others who are. It is unsettling and stressful when we or people we love are not well. When we are awakened, we view illnesses and imbalances differently than unawakened souls do. Though we are physically affected, mentally and emotionally we will work with the issue as we do with every other hump in life. An awakened soul does not get swept away by fear and is endowed with strength and peace beyond the physical in line with our spirit.

Generally, initial pain, illness, and disorder are the body's way of telling us that something is not right. If we ignore these signs long enough, the body has amazing abilities to adapt. It will start to accept these symptoms as normal until another crisis point where it signals us again through pain or illness. Pop a few pills and ignore the problem again, and it will continue until one day something major occurs. The body is unable to function in perpetual overdrive whether mentally, emotionally, or physically. Most chronic illnesses are based on the buildup of years of imbalances. We ignore them and don't feel them anymore until the body experiences a total breakdown. Then it is sometimes too late.

If, despite our best care at all levels of our being, we find ourselves facing an unexpected illness, we may initially be shaken. However, to the awakened this is another life event that our spirit will absorb. As spirit, we know that everything in life happens for a higher reason. If we are still and quiet, we may see the lessons, messages, and potential for growth beyond the immediate situation and follow our innate trust in our spirit to make the right choice toward recovery whether it is natural therapies, modern medicine, or both. In evaluating and making required changes, we will see the light toward the growth of our spirit and the spirits of those we love.

The awakened view illnesses and imbalances as any other tribulation in life. No human body is immune to all illnesses, imbalances, and imperfections. Though we might have done our best, we will feel the short and long-term effects of our polluted environment, the constant presence of electromagnetic waves, the continuous mutation of all microbes, the depletion of our soil and the inferior foods this produces, and the fast pace of modern life. Unless we segregate ourselves in a totally pure environment and have never ever neglected our bodies in the past, imbalances are a possibility.

Illnesses do not imply the deliberate intention of life to battle and destroy us. Sickness is sometimes a natural adjustment of survival mechanisms on an individual level or by a whole life cycle. Although on a personal level this may be unsettling, devastating, or traumatic, especially in the case of a fatal diagnosis, on a universal level, the life force must always adjust to balance itself. Human forms like any other life forms have life spans. Ideally, we would all like to end our lives peacefully and quietly in our sleep in full health without pain and suffering, at a ripe old age when we are ready to go. But we are only a speck in the big scheme of life, and our desires may be just as unrealistic as those of the unfortunate starving child who perishes on the plains of Ethiopia.

When we are an awakened spirit, upon a diagnosis we will initially allow every human emotion, be it hurt, sadness, anger, or fear. But as spirit we naturally transmute into peaceful understanding, acceptance, and integration. In the wisdom of quietude, we may find the clarity to work with the condition, taking the path toward change, treatment, and recovery. We flow with every wave in the sea of life, and this is just another wave. We will do best what we feel compelled to do with our innate spirit guiding us. We will have an innate trust that all will happen as it is meant to happen. Thus we will progress on our journey of treating the illness by working with the flow in total peace and enjoying every living moment with people we love as fully as we always do.

Many human minds tend to adopt a battle approach toward illnesses, especially cancer. The journey of cancer treatments is debilitating enough without adding such strong mental and emotional resistance. Andreas Moritz, a long-time Ayurveda natural medicine practitioner and healer, details clearly in his book *Cancer Is Not a Disease* the nature, causes, and attitudes toward this rising modern condition. Though viewed as controversial by modern medicine for which the cancer battle is big business, the facts put forward are essential from a holistic perspective. He presents the truth about the nature of the mind-body-spirit connection in any illness.

How we view our healing journey is our choice. Would we rather proceed with peace in our hearts on the path that feels right by our spirit, or would we rather do a tribal dance and expend all our energies on going to war with an imbalance that arose because of a disturbance to homeostasis in the first place? The first option will see less energy expended on mental, emotional, and physical turmoil and more directed toward our healing. Like mountaineers who battle their perception of a threat from the mountains they climb, those who battle cancer choose to expend their energies on a perceived enemy that is in fact a natural survival mechanism. Even if battle must be the choice, noting the wisdom described in Sun Tzu's *Art of War,* we would be better off fighting the enemy not by charging forward and battling force with force, but by deflecting his force and fighting back using his energy.

Concerning chronic illnesses and conditions, there is the tendency if we are not careful to fall into the trap of attachment through identification with whatever ailment we supposedly have. Medicine is big business. The pharmaceutical industry is second in size only to the food industry. To continue growing, the industry needs new conditions and illnesses to treat. A growing number of patients suffer from these once-unheard-of conditions. For example, more and more children are being diagnosed with attention deficit disorder and adults with depression, fibromyalgia, chronic fatigue, chronic migraines, obsessive-compulsive disorder, and eating disorders. Unless a disorder is acute and due to inflammation caused by a foreign microbe, bacteria, or an injury, almost all chronic conditions are simply an imbalance of mind, body, and spirit manifested physically.

Diagnosis is useful to indicate an imbalance, but our focus should be on attending to the root cause. We should be aware enough not to attach to a category or label and start living into our condition. These days it is not an exaggeration to say that depression is the diagnosis for every second or third person who goes through a low phase in life. If someone is down because a relationship has ended or because he is unable to handle the stresses of life, he will see a medical specialist and get prescriptions for antidepressants and sleeping pills and possibly sessions with a psychiatrist. He is told he has depression. Suddenly, he has a condition to identify with, not unlike a belief, attitude, or opinion. He talks a lot about his condition, thinks about it, starts to view everything through it, and validates his every move with it. Something that is part of the natural cycle of life becomes a larger-than-life reality and is a justification and cause for everything.

Instead of seeing a physical, mental, or emotional manifestation of imbalance as part of the bigger flow and attending to the root cause, we may start to fixate on the condition, consciously or unconsciously feeding it. Hence many find themselves dependent on medication or unable to improve despite years of treatment. This unawareness can cause the unawakened to be stuck forever in a vicious cycle. When we are an awakened spirit, we respect and heed the message and attend to the root cause true to our spirit. At the same time, we let go as we would relinquish anything that we are not.

This condition, illness, or phase is just another arising in us, but it is not us. These imbalances are part of the cycles just like everything else that arises. Does the root cause of our predicament lie in issues of unfulfillment, past woundings, disempowering thought patterns, or a disconnection with life through an unawakened spirit? We have been conditioned to believe that if we don't fix and mask our imbalances with strong medication, we will stay ill forever or die. That may be true to some extent, because if treatment for the imbalance is administered from the perspective of limited understanding and consciousness, and treatment is received from a limited understanding, it is simply a desperate bid to preserve the small self. Then yes, regardless of how much medication we consume or don't consume, we may remain ill and may not just die, but die in fear.

However, if we awaken and heal from the level of spirit, healing will naturally flow through all levels to our physical being. This is how many awakened souls have healed themselves in the past, and many who have learned to heal themselves have awakened to their spirit.

Medical science likes to shrug off this innate power as the "placebo effect" because when viewed from a limited, unawakened perspective it is ludicrous and unbelievable, and the limited human mind rejects anything that does not match its prescribed explanation, model, or theory. From the perspective and workings of our spirit, nothing in the physical world that arises stays static. It is part of a flow. It is our choice to fixate on a point that gets us stuck on it. By working from our spirit, we naturally do whatever we are compelled to do and seek aid from whomever and through whatever our spirit directs to rebalance and heal ourselves.

We will not use and attach to the label given to us to keep us in the role of helpless victim, totally identified and controlled by a seemingly overpowering condition. When we heal from the level of spirit filtering into emotional, mental, and physical, almost all chronic imbalances with their physical symptoms generally heal and disappear. True healing requires change and transformation in the light of our spirit wisdom. Then our suffering will end and we will be at peace.

There is a distinct difference between pain and suffering. Pain is a physical sensation we experience through our physical senses—our nerve endings. Suffering, however, is in the mind and emotions. Nelson Mandela endured years of physical imprisonment and torture but remained strong in spirit despite it all, without hate and vengeance but with compassion toward his captors. We can't force or fake that. Only someone true to his pure spirit is capable of such strength.

Let's consider two women, one unawakened and the other awakened. Both have been diagnosed with the same type of cancer and are undergoing the same course of chemotherapy, which has resulted in the same side effects of nausea, weight loss, hair loss, muscle pain, and weakness. The unawakened woman dislikes and despairs at the physical sensations of all those side effects, and battles the experience by getting angry and feeling victimized by life for "giving" her cancer. She faces anxiety and intense fear that the chemotherapy might not succeed. She suffers every day, not just physically but mentally and emotionally, and all her energy is depleted.

The awakened woman is saddened and shocked initially, but staying in her spirit, she makes peace with what is and what she must endure. She does not attach any thoughts, judgments, or resistance to her treatments or to the side effects. Even though she is ill and uncomfortable, she rests and meditates to help stay in her spirit and not get swept away by the intense physical sensations she feels. She has no fear because she knows that her true self can never die; only her body is going through this turbulence. She is not well physically, but she is at peace. She is not suffering.

We are extremely fortunate in the Western world with the advancement of health sciences that we can choose from variety of treatments and therapies. Natural health and medicine are growing industries, and people are increasingly choosing to use natural herbs and treatments to prevent and heal the root causes of imbalance, as opposed to using medication to mask symptoms. The evolution of treatments will naturally flow into vibrational and energy healing within a scientific framework in the move toward integrative medicine, with patients treated on every level of their being.

Biologist Bruce Lipton had said that allopathic modern medicine is outdated because it is based on Newtonian physics, the theory that the physical world consists of parts. When there is a problem, we separate the parts and treat them individually. With the growth in the science of quantum physics, what Albert Einstein once said has been proven: "The field is the sole governing agent of a particle." So why study just the particle when we should study the field? And why treat just the parts when we should also treat the whole? In natural medicine, ranging from naturopathy and herbalism to traditional Chinese medicine and Ayurveda, the patient is treated as a whole being, all systems and structures of the body are viewed as interconnected, and all levels of the being—mental, emotional, spiritual—are treated as an integrated whole.

Modern medicine has saved and improved many lives. These days it is common for life spans to extend into the seventies and eighties, especially in the advanced countries. The amazing reconstruction of body parts, from heart bypasses to knee replacements, has helped many. Modern medicine has successfully treated injuries and acute conditions. The path of treatment we select for illnesses or imbalances is a personal choice. If we are true to our spirit, we will take responsibility for our health by healing on all levels and keeping ourselves well informed to help make choices along the path. Science and spirituality are already converging. Many medical doctors are becoming more holistic and open, able to perceive the bigger picture, treating their patients using medical science with the underlying wisdom of mind, body, and spirit.

Natural therapies are being presented more scientifically to the public, are governed by more established professional standards, and have received recognition and acceptance by most private medical funds. Also, the successful application of science and technology has enabled the emergence of reliable means of obtaining information from our bodies and energy fields. These means include bio-resonance, mineral analysis, and iridology machines. Human intelligence, which continues to evolve, has produced new knowledge about the natural workings of mind, body, and spirit. New fields of treatment have emerged in herbalism, kinesiology, nutritional medicine, and many other areas, and all work in conjunction with each other.

Whatever choices we make with innate trust and knowing rooted in our own spirit are right for us alone whether it is the choice to go solely down the natural path, down the path of modern medicine alone, or a combination of both. If we awaken and stay true to our spirit in our journey of healing, then means in line with our choice will emerge. If we choose responsibility, empowerment, trust in self, information, and learning through an active approach, we will attract into our lives physicians and therapies from the awakened consciousness field. They will work in line with us, treating us as a whole being, not as parts of a machine. If we choose to stay ignorant, victimized, helpless, and passive and place the responsibility for our health in the hands of others for a quick fix or "you fix it" solution, we will attract into our lives physicians and techniques from the unawakened and unaware perspective and will simply get the means to mask our problem.

True healing can occur only through ourselves. Therapists and physicians, however impressive their credentials, are only part of the healing component. They simply provide aid, for we are the key to true healing. Any genuine therapist or physician knows that all paths toward recovery and healing involve the patient and therapist or physician working hand in hand. Again, as in all other areas, we have the choice.

Reflection

If you or someone close to you is undergoing a journey of healing with a particular illness or imbalance, evaluate where you stand and how you feel in the light of your awakened spirit. Evaluate the root cause of the imbalance on all levels of your being—mental, emotional, physical, and spiritual. Notice that you have choices in your journey of healing.

CHAPTER 15

Success and Wealth

WHAT IS SUCCESS AND WHAT is wealth? What images do the words *success* and *wealth* conjure up in our minds?

To an average middle-income individual in an economically developed country, these words might mean a chest full of glimmering gold coins. We might imagine sitting on a beach chair on a tropical island, sipping a piña colada, wearing a big grin, and leading a relaxed life with no worries in the world. These days the majority of people are driven by their material needs, their endless desires, dreams, and goals. Money-making seminars and investment clubs are a whole new industry that is growing in popularity like a new religion. The media portrays images of all sorts of material goods and services to appeal to the lack within, from tropical holidays to fancy cars and fine jewelry. Without awareness, we get brainwashed into believing that everything that can be purchased in this physical world defines our success, our peace, and happiness.

To a starving, homeless orphan in the slums of India, success and wealth probably conjure up images of a loving family and a job that provides income, a steady supply of food, a home, and sanitation. Success and wealth are relative and mean different things to different people in different environments at different points in time. Clearly success and wealth are subjective internal perceptions that contribute to the creation of our external physical reality, and not the other way around; an external object can't fulfill a lack in our internal state. This is why material wealth is subject to the law of diminishing returns. The more we have, the more we want, so when do we ever get enough?

Take the homeless orphan from the slums of India, give him all his desires—income, home, food, family—then ask him again two years later to outline his idea of success and wealth. This time he might say having a BMW and a big mansion and traveling the world with no need to work. Ask a man in an economically advanced country who has $5 million in his bank account and he might say success and wealth to him mean having $25 million. Clearly the idea of success and wealth is relative and changes like everything else in our material world.

Most individuals aspiring to success and wealth will tell you without a shadow of doubt that it is not the money they are fixated on, but what the money can buy—happiness and freedom. Success and wealth represent the intangible desires of our hearts for total freedom, the end to our suffering. So why are we suffering? Where is our suffering? Like illness, suffering is in our mind. It is not produced by other people or external circumstances, though we perceive it as being inflicted upon us. In the limited understanding of the unawakened, life is lived from the perspective of fear and lack within, hence endless wants and desires to try to stem the fear and fulfill the lack. There is an underlying fear of the unknown and not having enough and a lack from not knowing our true self. Thus self-fulfillment, joy, and peace cannot be derived from material sources.

When we awaken to our spirit, it will become clear that like all else in our physical existence, our perception has a major flaw. Many continue to live this illusion, either because they are ignorant or lack courage to make a change. Those who live the illusion have got it backward in believing that success and wealth are the means to freedom and happiness. In fact, it is our freedom and happiness independent of anything material that will result in success and wealth. Success and wealth are actually the results, not the means. Those who choose to labor under a misconception will remain stuck and never find enough success and wealth. They will be like a dog chasing its own tail. This flaw in perception is caused by living from the mind instead of the heart, the unfortunate state of the spirit in the unawakened. The mind analyzes, plans, schemes, and manipulates to get what it wants. It is ruled by fears of the past, and the present is consumed by fear of lack in the future. These fears are disguised as endless needs and desires.

The natural law of karma says that if what we send out is fear, lack, limitation, and heartlessness, then what returns is exactly the same. Our external world is a reflection of our internal self. The external will change only in response to changes in our inner self, not the other way around. Many find themselves constantly changing jobs and careers because of issues they perceive in a particular job or career when actually the issues are in themselves. Still unsorted and unresolved, the same issues resurface in different jobs and with different people.

When we awaken and live as spirit, we do not live from a contracted mind but flow with what feels intuitively right. If change in the external is required, our spirit will compel us to step into the unknown, let go of what is not right, learn, change, venture, and trust in its manifestation of new and endless possibilities. But we can have the courage and wisdom to see and make the choice only by living through the spirit.

Success entails wealth because wealth is a means of measuring and indicating success. Wealth may come in a variety of forms. In an advanced economy, it will take the form of cash in the hand and numbers on a bank account balance. In an economic depression, wealth might be loaves of bread or some potatoes. The currency of wealth is any form of exchange, and what it represents in the end is an exchange of energy. Regardless of what goods or services are offered, limited human beings with limited physical capacity put a certain amount of time and energy into producing and making them available, so wealth is a return for what is expended. Wealth to the minds of unawakened souls measures success only in tangible, physical forms of exchange because it indicates the amount others are willing to give in exchange for what we possess or the amount we have available to purchase whatever we desire to possess. However, success and wealth in the awakened spirit cannot be measured or indicated, because they are not just a tangible amount of exchange. They are an overflow of the inner abundance, fulfillment, and wholeness from the synchrony of our spirit with all of life.

Sometimes, as awakened souls we may misunderstand and feel guilty about accepting payment for our products and services, which we may feel are just an overflow from our spirit. However, if we have expended time, energy, and costs on training and education and on providing goods or services that others need, and if we have stayed true to our spirit and done this ethically, there should be no guilt in engaging in the process of exchange. Others are paying in exchange for the energy we have expended. At every point of the exchange and in deciding what to do with the results, we must take care to stay true to our spirit and not get swept up by greed and ego-based desires. Many well-known awakened teachers and gurus have gotten sidetracked when endowed with abundance from the universal overflow. By falling into the trap of the limited mind of ego, desires, greed, and hoarding, we will inevitably impede the natural flow of abundance from that universal plane and fall under the physical law of limitations, polarity, and instability. In time, the physical law of karma will catch up with us as well.

Some may be inclined to give without an immediate exchange, for instance through charity and humanitarian work. If such is our spirit's journey, we will honor that. Nature and the law of karma will return to us in abundance the inner fulfillment and growth of our spirit. That is how many aid and welfare workers have attested to the successes of their journeys.

When we are awakened and live as spirit, we have no fear, for we know that we are part of a universal reality that has an intelligence of its own. When we stay true to our spirit, we work in synchrony with life, and life is infinite and abundant. Life works out its own ways. Miracles happen and everything falls into place. Success, to the awakened, is living in line with this flow. As vessels, we have allowed life's infinite energies to channel through us. Staying true to our spirit, we will have the wisdom to channel the abundance in line with our spirit of unconditional love, compassion, and peace.

In terms of a successful and fulfilling career path, there is a difference between living our spirit's journey and living our human journey. In the awakened, living true to our spirit means following the passion of our hearts. Passion resides in the heart. Our spirit journey comes through our hearts. When we follow our hearts and live our passion, a natural synchronicity is felt deep in the heart center and flows through everything we do in line with that. When we pursue a path in tune with our spirit, we soar with an insurmountable joy. That path does not entail ego needs, attachments, or reasons. We are totally present in and flowing with the moment, with no intentions, let alone expectations. This naturally brings abundance in all areas.

Not living in line with our spirit, on the other hand, makes us feel like we are constricting and shriveling up on the inside. This out-of-sync feeling occurs when we make choices consciously or unconsciously based on egocentric needs, desires, attachments, expectations, and intentions. Seeing this allows us the courage and trust to make changes.

In following our passions, we must always maintain our trust and be open, for our paths could meander or deviate. Guided by our spirit wisdom and inner knowing, we will hear, see, and make choices accordingly. At all times, we must continue to allow the free flow of infinite creative energy through us. Many contented, successful people show evidence of doing this. When asked, they never say that their plan was to achieve fame or fortune. They simply lived their spirit's journey, following their hearts, and success, fame, and fortune were the by-products.

The infinite universal energy of abundance that flows through us exudes pureness, unconditional love, peace, and oneness and prompts giving, sharing, and creating. When we pursue success and wealth through manipulation, greed, hoarding, abuse, neglect, ignorance, or disempowerment and at the expense of other life forms, be they other humans, animals, or our living environment, we are not flowing with the universal infinite energy of life. Such success and wealth will be unstable and subject to the laws of the limited, physical, ego-based world. Again, natural karma will return to us the same energy we have projected out.

Reflection

View your life, possessions, desires, dreams, and goals. Examine if they are based on fear and lack within or an overflow of your inner abundance. Cultivate trust and flow with your spirit in all areas of work and creation, and your internal synchrony with life will automatically result in success on all levels in your external world.

CHAPTER 16

Aging and Death

THIS TOPIC WARRANTS A CHAPTER of its own because aging seems to be one of the biggest fears in any society. In addition to the material goods that we constantly purchase to fulfill some inner lack, an ageless and immortal body is one of our biggest desires, and we live the illusion that we can control our destiny. Why the fear of and resistance to aging? Because "beauty" and youth are signs of life and energy. And aging entails the biggest threat to the human psyche, the fear of nonexistence, the fear of death. This is a sad predicament because in the minds of the small, limited self, life started when we were born and ends when we die. However, the awakened know that life never began and most certainly will never end, so there is no fear.

While famine stalks some parts of our world and many wonder where they will get their next meal, in our all-too-affluent society, the priority for some seems to be spending fortunes on enhancing and sculpting our bodies. Many frequently visit cosmetic surgeons to get bits of our bodies cut off, foreign bits put in, and toxins injected into our faces. Some of us pump weights beyond our capabilities, compete in ultramarathons, summit high mountains, and run across vast deserts.

We take our bodies over the edge to prove to ourselves that we are still strong, youthful, able, and not growing older. We have an attachment to a desired external appearance and a fear and insecurity that lead us to fight the natural process of aging. People may say, "Oh, I know aging is normal, and I will grow old gracefully," but in the next breath, they will ask, "Do you think my chin and neck are saggy?"

We all know that the human body is mortal; it is born and it will die. The only certainty is that it will die one day, and the only uncertainty is the time and type of death. Like all other living organisms, the body has a cycle. From birth, our bodies and minds undergo growth through expansive energies, just like a seedling becomes a strong plant that flowers. This plant then gets old and withers, and as with us, its energy contracts back into itself toward the end of its physical life. Even stars and planets in the infinite space of our universe operate this way. Our choice to resist by artificially halting this process may provide temporary comfort, but reality will continue to run its course. When we awaken and live as spirit, we know our true self. Who we truly are is never born and can never die. Who we truly are is not in how we look but how we feel. This brief human life is only one of many and is just a journey to experience, learn, grow, create, and make a difference.

No one knows or can claim to know exactly what happens after the physical body dies, but based on near-death experiences and our current understanding of energies as life force, probable and possible assumptions can be made. Who we truly are beyond physical mind and body is spirit, essence, consciousness, energy. Whatever name we wish to use, we are without a doubt an experiential reality. The laws of science and physics have proven that energy cannot be destroyed, only transformed. So like the television set unplugged at the power source or the cadaver with living energy no longer surging through it, the living essence that is us never dies or ends but simply transforms. This is the basis for the Buddhist concept of reincarnation, which accounts for what may happen after the death of one physical form.

This concept matches many accounts by individuals from various cultures and parts of the world who have detailed memories and familiarity with or knowledge of places and people with no connection to their present lives. Perhaps reincarnation is the possibility most in line with the science of energy. Whether we choose to believe in reincarnation or the possibility of designated places called heaven for the good and redeemed and hell for the evil and condemned, what we know for sure when we experience the reality of our spirit is that the true self is infinite. It has no beginning and no end. Form came out of nothing and shall return to nothing, yet this nothingness is also a fullness. The journey of life feels like a journey out and then a return home, and birth and death are merely doorways.

But until we are fully realized, our essence chooses to manifest in form again and again to continue learning and evolving. Such is the innate longing of our spirit. So if we choose not to learn in this lifetime and leave many issues unresolved, our remaining layers keep our spirit energy in the heavier, denser, and agitated vibrational field and will choose many more lifetimes to learn.

The limited small-ego self lives in fear because the eternal spirit is not its reality. Many choose to resist the natural cycles of life and death. In life, we do everything physically possible to sustain our small self, for we perceive all that does not meet our desires and all who apparently differ as threatening our extinction. This ingrained fear in every unawakened being is the basis for discrimination, abuse, violence, and warmongering, all in the name of self-preservation. Self-preservation is for the small self. Our true self does not need preservation. It is the source of life and is life itself. It seeks to connect, not to destroy.

So we age. As the saying goes, "Change is the only constant in life." When we are spirit, our outer appearance is of little concern to us. Whether we have three little wrinkle lines or ten little wrinkle lines is of ridiculously amusing insignificance. The unawakened resist the physical changes that naturally occur with aging. The awakened embrace the natural progression of life while continuing to care for body, mind, and soul.

Engaging in energy arts like yoga, tai chi, and qigong restores and balances our life force. Playing sports or regularly taking a walk promotes blood circulation, lubricates our joints, and gives us a dose of fresh air and vitamin D from sunlight, increasing vitality and health. If we are totally present, enjoy every precious moment of each day, and connect with the natural life around us through giving, sharing, and receiving, we will keep happy hormones pumping through our blood, ensuring that our immune system stays strong. Maintaining an open mind to all beings and circumstances and living with compassion, tolerance, and wisdom will help produce a supple yet strong body.

An elderly person recently said, "The older I get, the more I find that life and our world are not black and white, but shades of gray." Some of us wisely choose to soften, yet many others don't. If we are health and vitality, we feel healthy, vital, and beautiful, and this translates naturally into looking healthy, vital, and beautiful. There are more experiences to be had, wisdom to impart, people to connect with, places to see, and lessons to learn regardless of how old we are.

The energy we expend and obtain by living from our hearts and infinite spirit continues to bring joy, laughter, and fun, making us feel forever young. This is what is meant by "young at heart" and "growing old gracefully." Awakened spirits exude pure, living energy through movement, love, a smile, laughter, words, and eyes, all of which, incidentally, tends to make us look younger. Unawakened souls expend endless energy on the limited self, worrying about and resisting the aging process, which makes them look and feel depleted.

Unawakened to our spirit and living with contracted, limited, fear-driven, disempowering thinking and conditioning, we fuel unhealthy toxic emotions that filter through to all areas of our lives and all parts of our bodies. All areas, from relationships to health, and all aspects of our body, from the minute cells to the skeletal posture, reflect the imbalance, which results in quicker aging. More cells die than are replenished, more energy is expended than restored, and there is more wear and tear than repair. Worse, if still unawakened on our deathbed, we may leave this world with fear. The awakened are already at peace. When and how the journey ends are honored, and they leave as a pure and peaceful vibration.

Reflection

Look into the truth of yourself, your life process, and the concept of death. Does any of these evoke fear in you? If so, continue on your spiritual journey with this awareness. In time, as you grow and mature, the continuous revelation of your spirit will bring the dissolution of all fears, including the fear of change, nonexistence, and death.

CHAPTER 17

Transformation

Be the change you wish to see in the world.
—Mahatma Gandhi

OUR WORLD IS IN CRUCIAL need of a major transformation from living as unawakened, contracted beings to living as conscious, awakened spirits in human form. This is possible if each of us chooses to embrace this transformation. This individual shift will then naturally become a collective global shift and move humankind into the awakened era.

When we live as a limited small self, our reality is confined within this physical mind, body, and world. Physical existence is limited and subject to all natural laws of the physical world—polarities, impermanence, and separation. Operating from this limited perspective, we will seek only to protect the self and everything in the world that goes toward sustaining this limited self. Fear, lack, greed, and distinction become the driving forces. This results in war, violence, abuse, manipulation, exploitation, and hoarding. Such is the destructive state of the human psyche that makes up a large part of our world today.

If we turn on the television or radio, our senses are bombarded with this sad reality. We consciously or unconsciously feed this dysfunction by playing on fear, greed, a sense of lack, and the quest for distinction through the power of political and economic structures, media, and communications. Thus individual dysfunction becomes global. This will inevitably lead to self-destruction. This is the state of blindness in which many individuals live. They are ignorant or lack courage to step out of this vicious cycle into the reality of what we truly are.

If we choose to remain fearful and ignorant, the natural course may see us destroying all life on earth including ourselves. Perhaps this will be the end of our world as we know it and the beginning of an unknown world. If, however, we have the courage to awaken and live our spirit path, transformation will come, heralding the end of an era of blindness and ignorance and the beginning of the era of conscious, awakened living.

Our world is experiencing increased suffering and chaos—a reflection of our collective internal state. We have forgotten who we truly are. Global transformation can occur only when each individual has the courage to awaken from this amnesia to our true self and then make choices true to our spirit. The human race is the only species on earth evolved enough to be capable of this privilege.

The widespread anxiety about end-of-the-world phenomena again plays on human fears and reflects the dysfunction of our perception as limited, separate selves under threat of extinction. When we know who we truly are, we know that life is infinite. It never had a beginning and will never have an end. Life continues in infinite cycles. We have intuitively known this from the beginning of human times. The symbol of life in all cultures, from the Celtic to the Tibetan, is infinity in various forms, all amazingly depicting no beginning and no end. Such symbols emanate from that infinite space that is the real us. Life will continue. It may express itself in various forms or nonforms, but it will always find a way to endure. Try pulling out weeds and they continue to grow; kill germs with antibiotics and they mutate. Life transforms but cannot end. According to the Mayan elders, the prophesied end of times actually means the end of an era and the beginning of another. We are the ones with the choice to determine this. Whatever it is, we—life itself, essence—will continue in some form.

It is an exciting time as many souls are awakening and evolving each day, leading the collective consciousness level toward a critical mass. Many are instilled with courage and will no longer sit back and shake their heads or throw their arms up in the air in hopelessness. They have chosen to stop feeding on collective fear by turning off the sensationalized bad news on their televisions and radios, online chat rooms, and social media, instead connecting with real life and making a difference. They have chosen to awaken, heal, and transform. Many awakened souls live among us, but until we ourselves awaken, we may be oblivious to them, as we see only within our limited perceptions. But once we awaken, we tune in to this higher vibration. When we become awakened souls, every word, action, and thought we project will be infused with spirit energy. Just one enlightened spirit's higher energy has the ability to transmute the lower vibrations of a mass of dysfunctional souls. This higher frequency and vibration of our collective existence can heal and balance our planet and all us living beings who cohabit on it.

When we awaken to our spirit, to the reality of who we truly are beyond this physical mind and body, we are whole, perfect, divine, and eternal. Unconditional love and peace, oneness, and abundance flow from us, and we have the freedom of choice and the power to create. We have more energy and capacity to enjoy, create, share, and experience. This seemingly idealistic reality is possible globally because the reality of this true self is within all of us, but awakening starts within each of us. Through individual awakening, change can filter into our family, friends, neighbors, community, and the world. As in all areas, it is through the shift internally that the shift can occur externally. It begins here and now with us and within us.

Reflection

We cannot make a dark room any less dark simply by sitting there, doing nothing. But when we light a candle or become the little flame on the candle, the light from the little flame will banish the darkness. Ask yourself where you stand. What is your role? Do you have the courage to wake up to your true self and make choices in line with your spirit?

Afterword

INNER PEACE, JOY, AND FULFILLMENT independent of anything in our material world, including all perceptions of ourselves, are possible if we are open to see and have the courage to let go of all that we are not, revealing our true self, our spirit, and essence. We must shift our focus to what is real in us—the ever-present quiet and stillness—and away from all the noise and movement.

To awaken to our true self is a privilege that filters through into all areas of our physical being and world. If we are anchored in what we truly are, the journey of life provides opportunities for learning, growth, and evolution of our spirit into its full realization.

Be open, hear and see, and allow the spirit to awaken. Then trust in that experience and continue the journey of letting go. At every point in our journey, we are free to choose until we are spirit in a human form. Then a journey of an amazingly different kind begins. The journey and the flow continue through fractals and are infinite. Such is the gift and beauty of the ultimate freedom.

APPENDIX

Breath Meditation

FIND A COMFORTABLE POSITION IN a comfortable place where you will not be disturbed for at least ten minutes. You may increase your meditation time gradually as you practice regularly and find the exercise easier. Choose a time that is convenient for you, whether early in the morning, at lunchtime, or in the evening before retiring for the night. It should be a time when you can be alone, without distractions from people, excessive noise, and other activities.

Sit on the floor (cross legged) or with your back against a wall (if you have a serious back problem or pain), or sit upright on a chair or lie supine on the floor. If lying supine is your preference, ensure that you will not drift off to sleep, for then you will not be meditating. Ensure that your spine is relaxed but upright, not slouched, to ensure efficient flow of energy up and down the spine. Wear loose, comfortable clothing, and if the weather is cold, wear warm clothes, a rug, or shawl, because the body's temperature drops during total relaxation. Minimize distraction as much as possible. Distracting body sensations may be one of the biggest challenges for a beginner in meditation.

Once you are in a comfortable position, close your eyes gently and remain as still as possible for the duration of the meditation.

1) With eyes closed, body still and relaxed, take three deep breaths. Imagine all tension leaving your body with each of three deep out-breaths. Then let go, settle, and let the breath do its own thing. Simply observe your breathing. Focus on where you feel your breath the most. Your breath may be sensed most in the expansion and contraction of the chest or diaphragm; it may be sensed in the nostrils as fresh air flows in and out; it may be sensed in the sound your breath produces in your skull. Stay with the most appealing sensation.

2) Allow the breath to take its own course and do its own thing. Simply be an observer, staying always just with the sensation of the breath. Your breath might be faster initially, then slow down; it might be deep or shallow. Allow and observe without controlling.

3) Mind chatter will start to intrude because when you are still and quiet, without the other physical senses engaged, thoughts appear louder and more distracting. This is especially true for a beginner in meditation. Again, simply allow and observe.

4) Remember you are not your thoughts, and the more attention you give them, the louder and stronger thoughts get. Even resistance is a form of attention. The more you resist something, the more you reinforce it. Simply remain the detached observer and direct attention again and again to the central focus of the breath, be it the chest, nostril, or skull.

5) Remain like an observer at a train station. Let all the trains come in and go out, in one ear, out the other. Do not hop on any of the trains; do not get swept away with any thoughts. Deal with them later. For now, you are just a neutral observer, staying strongly focused on your breath.

6) In the beginning, there may be many times when you find yourself wandering off and being swept away by thoughts, some distracting sensation in the body like pain or numbness in the legs, or noises in your surroundings. It does not matter. Calmly keep drawing yourself back to the point of focus, the breath. Continue to stay, allow, and observe.

7) Remain in this place until you feel ready to emerge from the meditation. When you are ready, take three deep breaths, wiggle your fingers and toes, and slowly open your eyelids.

If you are meditating for the first time, it is normal to find remaining focused on the breath challenging. But like every new skill, the more you practice, the easier it becomes. The easier it becomes, the more you will lose the concept of time. Many regular meditators find a thirty-minute sitting feels like five minutes. During times of physical or emotional turbulence and trauma, the mind noise and body discomfort may seem more powerful and intense, but the same principle applies. The more skilled you become at keeping your point of focus, the fainter and quieter everything else appears until at times it is almost as if nothing is there, not even your breath. Then there is simply you.

Glossary

samsara: The process of coming into existence as a differentiated, mortal creature.

bodhisattva: A person who has attained prajna, or enlightenment, but who postpones nirvana to help others attain enlightenment.

nirvana: A Buddhist term for state of enlightenment and end of suffering.

mantra: An often-repeated word, formula, or phrase, often a truism, chanted or sung as an incantation and prayer.

karma: Action seen as bringing upon oneself inevitable results, good or bad, either in this life or in a reincarnation.

shamanism: Spiritualism of the Native American Indian.

chi: The Chinese term for the vital life force in the body.

prana: "Breath," the body's vital energy.

chakra: Major energy centers in the body.

tai chi: A Chinese system of slow meditative physical exercise for relaxation and health.

qigong: A Chinese system of breathing and exercise to benefit mental and physical health.

meridians: Energy pathways in the body used in acupuncture and traditional Chinese medicine.

nadis: The term commonly used in yogic science to refer to the body's energy pathways.

Recommended Reading

Aitken, Robert. *Taking the Path of Zen*. New York: North Point Press, 1982.

Batchelor, Stephen. *Buddhism Without Beliefs: A Contemporary Guide to Awakening*. London: Bloomsbury Publications, 1997.

Chopra, Deepak. *Ageless Body, Timeless Mind: The Quantum Alternative to Growing Old*. New York: Harmony Books, 1993.

Cousens, Gabriel. *Spiritual Nutrition: Six Foundations for Spiritual Life and the Awakening of the Kundalini*. California: North Atlantic Books, 2005.

Dale, Ralph Alan. *Sacred Texts: The Tao Te Ching Lao Tzu (A New Translation, Commentary & Introduction by Ralph Alan Dale)*. London: Watkins Publications, 2002.

Desikachar, T.K.V. *The Heart of Yoga: Developing a Personal Practice*, rev. ed. Rochester: Inner Traditions International, 1999.

Gawain, Shakti. *Living in the Light*. California: New World Library, 1986.

Guo, Bisong. *Listen to Your Body: The Wisdom of the Dao*. Honolulu: University of Hawaii Press, 2001.

Hanh, Thich Nhat. *Peace Is Every Step: The Path of Mindfulness in Everyday Life*. London: Bantam Books, 1991.

Hay, Louise L. *You Can Heal Your Life*. Santa Monica, California: Hay House, 1982.

His Holiness the Dalai Lama. *How to See Yourself as You Really Are: A Practical Guide to Self Knowledge*. USA: Rider, 2008.

His Holiness the Dalai Lama. *The Art of Living: A Guide to Contentment, Joy & Fulfillment*. London: Thorsons, 2001.

Iqbal, Afzal. *The Life and Work of Jalaluddin Rumi*. USA: Oxford University Press, 1999.

Kornfield, Jack. *The Wise Heart: Buddhist Psychology for the West*. USA: Rider, 2008.

Kornfield, Jack. *After the Ecstasy, the Laundry: How the Heart Grows Wise on the Spiritual Path*. New York: Bantam Books, 2000.

Murphy, Susan. *Upside-Down Zen: Finding the Marvelous in the Ordinary.* Boston: Wisdom Publications, 2006.

Moritz, Andreas. *Timeless Secrets of Health & Rejuvenation: Breakthrough Medicine for the 21ˢᵗ Century.* USA: Ener-Chi Wellness Press, 2009.

Myss, Caroline. *Anatomy of the Spirit: The Seven Stages of Power & Healing.* London: Bantam Books, 1997.

Sheldrake, Rupert. *A New Science of Life.* Los Angeles: J.P. Tarcher, 1981.

Suzuki, Shunryu. *Zen Mind, Beginner's Mind: Informal Talks on Zen Meditation & Practice.* Boston & London: Shambala, 2011.

Tolle, Eckhart. *The Power of Now: A Guide to Spiritual Enlightenment.* Sydney: Hachette Aust, 2004.

Tolle, Eckhart. *A New Earth: Awakening to Your Life's Purpose.* Victoria: Penguin Group, 2005.

Wallace, B. Alan. *Contemplative Science: Where Buddhism & Neuroscience Converge.* New York: Columbia University Press, 2007.

Wallace, B. Alan. *Balancing the Mind: A Tibetan Buddhist Approach to Refining Attention.* New York: Snow Lion Publications, 2005.

Wolf, Fred Alan. *The Spiritual Universe: One physicist's vision of spirit, soul, matter and self.* Portsmouth: Moment Point Press, 1999.